MARION HALLIGAN

WORDS FOR LUCY

A STORY OF LOVE, LOSS AND THE CELEBRATION OF LIFE

For Bianca Lucy and Edgar James
Beautiful grandchildren

First published in Australia in 2022
by Thames & Hudson Australia Pty Ltd
11 Central Boulevard, Portside Business Park
Port Melbourne, Victoria 3207
ABN: 72 004 751 964

thamesandhudson.com.au

Most of the photographs in this book were taken by Graham Halligan, using a rather good camera he bought when studying in Europe on a scholarship in the 1950s.

25 24 23 22 5 4 3 2 1

Thames & Hudson Australia wishes to acknowledge that Aboriginal and Torres Strait Islander people are the first storytellers of this nation and the traditional custodians of the land on which we live and work. We acknowledge their continuing culture and pay respect to Elders past, present and future.

ISBN 978-1-760-76220-9 (paperback)
ISBN 978-1-760-76226-1 (ebook)

A catalogue record for this book is available from the National Library of Australia

Cover photograph: Lucy Halligan, aged seven, taken by Graham Halligan

Cover design: Sandy Cull
Typesetting: Cannon Typesetting
Editing: Alexandra Payne

Printed and bound in Australia by McPherson's Printing Group

FSC® is dedicated to the promotion of responsible forest management worldwide. This book is made of material from FSC®-certified forests and other controlled sources.

CONTENTS

WORDS FOR LUCY

MY DAUGHTER LUCY died on 10 November 2004, in the morning, at the age of thirty-eight.

She lay on her bed for a sleep, with her cat beside her, and her heart stopped. It was, I like to think, a death of her own manner and choosing, though I doubt she did this consciously.

My business is words. I put these together, my words, hers, other people's, in celebration of her life and of our grief for her loss of it, and ours of her. Not all the words are about her, but they are all for her.

~

Love is so important to us. We so much need it. We can't do without it. What we don't realise at the beginning is the price it comes at. When we kiss the lover, when we marry the beloved, when we nurse the child, there is such perfection, such joy, we do not know the cost that is beginning to be incurred, and the paradox that the greater the love the greater the price. Though, I do think a child often comes with fear; fear skulks through the wide open door of joy, it casts its shadow and a little shiver chills us, even if we don't entirely recognise it. Until the day of reckoning comes.

The price is loss. I have lost my husband, and my daughter. As I write these words in 2004 – it's not that date any longer, this book will have been eighteen years in the writing, such things don't come easily, you have to wait for them – I have a son, I have a new husband. I am building up further dreadful debits and may one day be asked to pay them. I say to my son, Make sure you don't die for a long time, and he promises. But he can't be sure. John, the husband, is several years younger than me, and very fit. But one of us will lose the other, one day.

You could choose to live without love and then there never would be loss. But who would want to do that?

Love equals loss. But it takes a while to twig.

I see my son James becoming aware of such things. He pays attention to me, I am his only close relative left. When I die there will be nobody at all of the generation before him, he will occupy that rather chilly eminence of the oldest in the family. There is an uncle by marriage, no aunts, some younger cousins who are all quite attached to one another but not in close contact because of geography, and it is much the same for his partner, she has a lot of cousins but not nearby. He is hanging on to me, and I am supposed to hang on to myself. But I sniff the air of mortality.

At the end of 2016, as we were waiting for his son to be born at seven o'clock the next morning, James informed me that I had to live another twenty years to see my grandson into adulthood. Mm. I doubt that is going to happen.

BEGINNINGS

Memoir | 2021

This memoir isn't very chronological. It doesn't start at a beginning and go through to an end. As you might imagine a photo album, beginning with birth, through babyhood, being a toddler, school, growing up, and so on and on. No, time and memory seldom travel together. When I wrote my family saga novel *Lovers' Knots* I was interested in getting the content of a saga without the massive proportions, and I came up with the image of a box of photographs. You pick them out at random, and so the story is told. This memoir is another such box of snapshots. You find your own way through the story, from random details.

That said, it does begin with Lucy's birth.

Tasting the air | 1966

When Lucy was born she tasted the air. She had a round little golden head – later doctors said she was jaundiced but when she was born she was golden, and very pretty, with smooth cheeks and no wrinkles or jowls. She lay in her crib on her back, put out her tongue and tasted the air. Very thoughtfully, as though she was testing this new medium that she found herself in. Quite voluptuously; she was offering herself a sensuous experience.

She seemed quite healthy then, though tired after a long labour, from early one morning to about three o'clock the next. It was another day before they decided she had a problem, and took her to the premmie nursery and put her in a thing called a Crown Street box, which was a five-sided cube of a kind of perspex, a bit bigger than her head, into which oxygen was fed. That was when the doctor, who was a practising Catholic, said, If you believe in having babies christened, then christen this one. We didn't believe in it, but we did christen her. Maybe to keep terror at bay; we knew what his words meant. It seemed important that some small ceremony should mark her short life. The archdeacon who had married us came from the church of St John's, a church much older than Canberra, belonging to the nineteenth-century homestead of Duntroon, and baptised her. Perhaps he thought we were afraid of her getting lost in limbo.

The premmie nurses decided she wasn't any good at breastfeeding and got her on to bottles, with my milk expressed. When James was born he did exactly the same thing, he choked and gagged and couldn't take the milk. I was heartbroken, and suddenly back in that terrible time when we thought Lucy was going to die. I panicked, and wept, it was all happening again. But then a wise nurse looked and said, The poor little mite is being drowned. She made me lie on my back so that the milk did not flood out and make the baby choke, and we did that for a good twelve months. I organised myself so I lay on the sofa or the bed, holding a book in one hand, the same arm cradling James, the other hand holding the nipple so he could suck comfortably. We spent vast amounts of our days, and at first nights, lying around like this, having a lovely time.

And I realised that if Lucy hadn't been in the premmie nursery, or if there had been a nurse wise in the ways of feeding babies, we would have worked out that Lucy's problem was not that she couldn't suck, but that she was being drowned, and so choked. She could have been breastfed. It is one of the sorrows of my life that she wasn't. I think she needed to be, I think she might have been less anxious in her childhood and adult life if she had had that long loving comfort. It might have given her a useful bulwark against the fearsomeness of hospitals and medical procedures. A suckling baby lies, and dozes, and drinks a bit, taking just as long as anybody will let her. But a bottle-fed baby, there it is, drink up, all gone, that's it. And other people want to do it. They like to think they are helping you, but it would be better if they did the dishes, and left this important task to you.

I am not a person given to regrets. I know they are pointless, what has happened is, it cannot be undone. But I cannot stop myself regretting that Lucy was not breastfed. For my sake, of course, the convenience of it. But I would not still regret that, forty years later. It is the comfort and the cosseting, the long lazy times spent in this milky haze of mutual delight, that I am so sad she missed.

At three weeks old she was flown to Melbourne, to the children's hospital. It was thought that I shouldn't go, that it would be too much for me. The cardiac physician did not think the breastfeeding mattered, he said that she would be better off staying with bottles. Until then I had thought that as she got older and stronger perhaps she would be able to cope with it. No, he said, you are only distressing yourselves. He was wrong, I know now, we could easily have done it. My milk drying up was one of the most agonising things ever to happen to me. I was ill for some time. And it wasn't just the physical response, it was sorrow for the loss of something that I believed was so essential for the both of us. Physically, Lucy thrived on bottles. But I think that, psychologically, she missed out.

The specialist in Melbourne (the Canberra GP had wanted Sydney, the pediatrician Melbourne; the senior man won, which was harder work for us over the years, since Sydney is much easier to get to) looked at her and said, Well, she has got a pretty funny heart, but she's okay, she's managing. We'll keep an eye on her, that's all. He did that, for nine years, and then she needed her first open-heart surgery. These days they would have done it much earlier and it might have all worked better, but that is not something one can dwell on. The very best was done, it was all quite pioneering, she was one of the oldest patients with her condition, the others hadn't survived.

Dr Venables, the cardiac pediatric physician, was able to make a more precise diagnosis than the funny heart. She was born without a pulmonary valve. This meant that when her heart pumped blood to her lungs there was no valve to close and keep it there. Her heart compensated, pumped extra hard to make up for what gushed back. But the result was an enlarged heart, and a very much enlarged pulmonary artery, so her lungs were compromised by this. The solution, to fix in place a tanned valve, in this case a pig's, was considered better left until she was as big as possible, since it wouldn't grow with her. It had to be replaced when she was twenty-one because it had calcified; apparently this is normal, teenagers produce a lot of calcium. The second time it was a tanned human valve. The valves worked well, it was the much enlarged pulmonary artery that was the problem.

When she was born, my husband had two nuns in his class. He was a lecturer at the Australian National University in Canberra at the time. Oh, Graham, one said, I see you have named your daughter for two child martyrs. Lucy Beatrice. Of course that wasn't our intent, we liked the names for their beauty and meaning.

~

When she was something less than six months old we went to Cambridge for some months. When we had announced to my parents that we were going to have a baby, they were less thrilled than I'd expected. We thought you were going overseas, they said. Oh yes, we replied, we'll still do that. And we did. We sailed on *Himalaya*, which was great fun. There's a photo of Lucy sitting in one of the lounges in a leather armchair of a dull turquoise colour. I remember how we'd prop her up to get her properly supported but how she'd always wriggle and then she'd fall over, in slow motion, sliding sideways in the chair, laughing as she went. They had a child-minding device on the boat, the switchboard would listen in to the cabin and if she stirred would call us; we always told them where we'd be. It was a comfort, but not often called on; once she went to sleep she stayed there. Late at night we'd go dancing, possibly in the bar called The Boot and Crampon. At midnight the boat would take its stabilisers in so it could go faster and then it would move quite dramatically from side to side and all the dancers would slide across the floor. Exhilarating.

In Cambridge we had a flat belonging to King's College, because Graham was a member of the college. It was on Barton Road, not many rooms but spacious and expansive with a pantry as big as a small bedroom and a gas stove that belonged in a museum. I met a young woman with a baby about the same age who lived in a flat in the block next door, her husband taught at the choir school; she had frozen damp on her walls. We didn't. I think we got more sun than she did. I wasn't familiar with damp, let alone frozen damp. We had a small apple orchard out the back, the fruit had the moth but I'd cut the damaged bits out and stew the rest. At one stage Lucy would eat anything if it was mixed with apple puree. I fed her a good bit of liver like that. We bought a car for fifty pounds, a sludge-coloured Standard Vanguard, built like a tank. You could stand up in the back and change the baby's nappy. She travelled either in a bassinet on the back seat or in a little white metal chair from Mothercraft that sat over the front bench seat. She could see out the windscreen and that amused her. You could also put it over a chair and make a high chair out of it. Now the dangerousness of this driving horrifies me, but then it seemed clever and safe. We drove to Italy in that car and left it with Ian, an Englishman there. Ian said he'd send us ten pounds if it went well but he never did. There were terrible penalties for abandoning a car in Italy so we supposed he'd at least sent in the papers to change the ownership. He was a playwright, later we saw some of his work on the television.

Sometimes from Cambridge we used to go to little lost churches and rub brasses, you still could in those days, now they have imitation ones set up in village halls. I suppose so the originals don't get worn out. One afternoon we set out to do a couple, the lord and his lady, she with a little dog under her feet, he with an equally small lion. Was it Sir John de Creke and Lady Aylene, at Westley Waterless? We had it on the wall for decades, but the silverfish ate it, and it is gone now. My brother-in-law Fred, to whom we gave Sir Roger de Trumpington, had him mounted on thin board and he is as good as ever.

We had a kind woman, a former Cambridge bedmaker, who came and babysat Lucy; she loved her dearly and they were both happy with this arrangement. We got to the church at about three o'clock on a November day, and it was already getting dark, especially in the dim old building. When the rector came in, we asked if we could have a light on. He was very grumpy, and said, Why hadn't we come at a reasonable hour instead of leaving it so late? We explained that we had a baby, and that she'd been asleep, and we'd had to get a babysitter, so then he felt sorry for his churlishness and put the lights on, explaining how money was tight, and the church kept decaying, and please make sure we turned them off. When we finished, Graham went out and put the car lights on, shining them on the door, and I turned off the church lights and stumbled out. We put ten shillings in the church roof box.

It wasn't a white Christmas in Cambridge that year but it was exceedingly wintry, and Christmas light and colour shone out against the gloom. I remember walking around with Lucy sitting on my arm and saying, Isn't that pretty, and that was her first word, pretty, pretty,

My passport photo from the time of the Cambridge trip, 1966.

spoken with a kind of breathless delight. She was a very pretty baby, and to see this pretty child saying pretty was such a pleasure.

We had a large Australian pram which could be used as a pusher, with flaps and roofs and all sorts of complicated mechanisms to fold it up. People were always stopping us and asking where could they buy one. English prams were the sort of grand carriage you see pictures of nannies pushing in parks. I've often told the story of going to Canterbury in the car, leaving the pram outside a teashop while we had a cup of tea, it was far too big to take inside, and then walking cheerfully to the car over the road without giving the pram another thought. When we got back to Cambridge and realised, we were in a panic, we didn't want to lose it. We rang up the Canterbury police who were rather worried too; a pram without a baby suggested a kidnapping. Next day Graham went on the train to get it and ended up coming through London at rush hour with this flogging great pram, standing up on tube trains clutching it.

A couple of times I caught the bus from the flat into town but it was really too hard, having to hold the baby in one arm while trying to fold the hefty great thing with the other, then heave it on to the bus. Even worse coming back with the shopping. I don't think those cute little umbrella pushers were around then, but when I saw one I wished they had been.

There was a good market in Cambridge. You could get excellent vegetables, including Fen celery, which was about half as long as we were used to, pale and crisp and fine. There was a game shop; once I bought a chicken, an ordinary chicken, and when we came to eat it found a whole lot of shot in it. We made jokes about game chicken and the shooting season. We wondered if a fox had attacked the henhouse and the farmer had shot it and got one of the chickens as well, or instead. Luckily we didn't break any teeth.

~

We'd planned to spend the last month or so of our time away in France but we couldn't find anywhere at all to live. We heard about an apartment in Alassio, not far from the Italian border with France. It was a kind of granny flat, the ground floor of a very grand villa with soaring ornamental iron staircases and black and white marble floors. The villa was at the top of an extremely steep and terraced garden, with geraniums and highly coloured flowers, though on the January day we moved in it snowed. The flat was narrow and long, partly excavated into the hill. It had a gas boiler in the kitchen called a Vesuvio and one in the bathroom, over a deep little sitz bath, called a Volcano, neither of which I found reassuring. We sometimes got mail for Tringham Reverend Arold, the father of the Englishman we were renting the flat from. It had been his apartment before he died. It had a pretty little fireplace where we burnt olive cuttings when we could afford them. They scented the air. There's a photograph of Lucy sitting on the hearth, in red leggings and a little red tartan top of the kind called I believe an angel jacket, holding an orange high in her hand and laughing at it. Mireille Mathieu was all the fashion then, she was always on the radio, and Lucy used to dance on her bottom to her singing, very energetically.

A couple of years ago we were going by train from Portovenere to Nice, a rather roundabout route because of the devastation in the Cinque Terre, the floods and mudslides, and the train stopped at Alassio. I peered out, nothing was familiar, not from the trip forty-five years ago when Ian the English playwright drove us to the station in the sludge-coloured Standard Vanguard soon to be his, which we put in the parking area on the other side of the tracks before we crossed the line and went into the large glittering cafe with its steamed-up glass doors and bought him a vermouth. Alassio in the nineteenth century had been an English town and still was in 1967 to an extent, with an English library as well as its streets lined with mandarin trees. The Hanbury family, which had owned most of the town and given its name to the main street, the Viale Hanbury, sold the land to the railways to build the station, with the proviso that the express train to Rome would always stop there if required. So we had arranged that, and stop it did, at ten o'clock at night, and not again as I recollect till we got to Rome. And then after a couple of days on to Naples and the boat home.

When our latter-day train stopped in the many-platformed busy station, I wondered if you could still order the Rome express to stop. I couldn't imagine it.

There was a kind of servant who came with the villa, a very jolly lady who would have done for us but we couldn't afford her. She spoke no English. She used to poke Lucy and say, Genoeve, Genoeve, and it turned out that she thought that was her name. She'd pat her tummy and say *boggia*, which we discovered was a dialect word; it became part of our family vocabulary, and now my granddaughter Bianca knows it. We walked around a lot with our baby in the pram. She wore a pretty little white quilted and hooded anorak that came from Mothercare over woollen leggings and various layers of woolly clothes, and had a beautiful cream-coloured wool shawl knitted by my aunt tucked around her. She was very cosy, I could tell when I slid my fingers in against her neck, she was wonderfully warm. Lucy was always a very warm child. But Italian little children used to wear so many clothes that they looked like tiny Michelin men and couldn't move for padding, their arms stuck out sideways, if they'd fallen over they'd have rolled around, so the relative svelteness of Lucy offended their elders. Women were always coming up to us and shouting, *bambina fredda, bambina fredda* – cold baby, cold baby – and we'd smile and shake our heads but they'd get very cross and repeat themselves. I didn't have the Italian to refute their claims. Graham would shake his head and say, No, she isn't. And in fact through all of that trip she was very healthy, that funny heart worked well for her, and we didn't need our letter to a heart specialist at the children's hospital in Great Ormond Street.

In Alassio we would buy chickens with their heads on so they had their innards in too, so we could feed Lucy the livers. We almost never bought Italian baby food, it was astronomical in price. She was still keen on apple puree, but she'd eat vegetables too, and a little chicken. I had a baby Mouli and pureed food through that. We did not travel light. We'd sent two tea chests of stuff to Southampton for the boat, plus trunks, and a large trunk from Alassio to Naples. The flat in Cambridge didn't have any kitchenware or plates, so we'd had to buy all that. I got six wonderful orange enamel plates – it was the sixties – at a posh department store in Cambridge, and they are still as new; I love them. And some brown Arabia fireproof ware. That was a wonderful period for design, original, and exciting, not a pastiche of earlier ideas. We'd taken our own linen and towels. It's odd to think of that, now we travel so light by air.

It was a good voyage home, nineteen days from Naples to Sydney via the Suez Canal, in *Oriana*, a most elegant ship. There was an awning stretched over one of the high decks and a bunch of us, young women with babies, sat there and played with them. That was an idyllic time, long watery tropical days, full of sun and sea air, nothing to do but play with babies. One of the young women was married to Lionel Long, the singer; she had a little girl a bit older than Lucy and we were good shipboard friends. Lionel and Graham hatched a plan for Graham to translate some French troubadour songs, which Lionel would sort out music for and sing, but nothing came of it. Graham was a committed perfectionist, and I think he was often reluctant to do things if he thought they would not meet his standards. When I started writing he was seriously worried: what if it didn't work, what if it had been done before? I think these were ways of fearing I would not be good enough. If you don't do things they can't fall short. Whereas, like a lot of writers, I was prepared to just do it and hope for the best. All writing equals risk.

A buffet lunch was set up on trestle tables on the deck so we didn't have to go inside. Lucy would have a nap in the afternoon and I could read. Indeed an idyllic time. There was a library, very quiet, where Graham could work. That was the very end of sea travel as a means of getting from place to place. Already the passengers were deeply divided, between those who were sailing because they wanted to go to Australia and those who were cruising for the fun of it, from Southampton to Southampton, at considerable expense of time and money. Each group rather despised the other, and considered what they were doing was the only proper thing. And you can imagine the age difference, youngish energetic working people with children, and the elderly cruisers.

In England I had bought some pieces of very cheap dress material and one of those Vogue Designer patterns, this one by Yves Saint Laurent. I had two dresses made in Alassio, by a woman who worked in a sort of vaulted cellar space in some kind of industrial building where I went for several fittings. She had a large gas bottle on a frame, with a mantel, that roared away in these vast chilly spaces to keep us warm, but only if you stood right in front of it. It worried me. I think I was frightened when I was little by one of those gas water heaters that you had to light with a match and that went *whooomp* and then roared. She made the dresses beautifully, and one evening on the ship I was wearing one of them, a dark red granny print covered with tiny flowers, sitting at the bar, when John Olsen, another returning Australian, touched it gently and said, Splendid dress. And so it was. But as I have remarked in other writing, I was twenty-six, and when you are twenty-six many dresses are splendid.

A commonplace

It's a commonplace that some catastrophe happening to a child, her death, or damage, a birth defect or an accident, can destroy the parents' marriage. Several times I have written such an outcome in fiction, because I have seen it so often. So looking back I have always been impressed that nothing like that ever happened to Graham and me, not even nearly. We were both committed to Lucy, and knew we were in it together, that we needed each other to get through our problems. Graham was always tender, and supporting; he did everything that could be done to help us get through our difficult times. I have a huge folio of memories of us in different hospitals, clinics, surgeries, waiting, always waiting, dreary, hopeful, hopeless, our chests heavy, holding hands sometimes. It was very painful for a long time because Lucy so hated the whole thing, she would cry. You could try to explain to her that an electrocardiogram wouldn't hurt, she might slightly believe you but still she'd cry, and it was quite certain that a great many of the procedures, needles, catheters, the whole business of blood-taking, were horribly painful. She got very brave, but always she hated it. And even when there were not physical procedures but just consultations, there was always the possibility of hurt from bad news.

I remember once when we were in a clinic in Melbourne there was a couple there, much older than us, with a girl of about thirty; they would even so not have been young when she was born. She had problems with her heart, but others as well. She couldn't talk, or sit up, she wasn't toilet trained. She was a small adult in size, but with the capacities of a baby not even a year old. She was called Eunice. She was capricious and difficult, but apart from showing her anger she did not communicate with her parents. We could see that they were bewildered by their plight, caring for a baby for whom nothing had changed in thirty years, except that she grew bigger and unmanageable. Changing the nappies of a small but vengeful adult. We knew we were so lucky in comparison, with Lucy's wit, and humour, her lively personality, her sunniness, her delight in the world, her lovingness. We had a go at talking to them but they had nothing to say. They had the blankness of despair.

I sometimes remembered when Lucy was born and the doctors suggested she was going to die and how passionately I wanted her to live, how I longed to keep this child, to not lose her, and how painful the prospect of that loss was, and how I couldn't bear it, knowing that I might have to and wondering how I ever could. And then, in her last years, I thought about that, if it might have been easier for her if she'd died as a baby. I would have had to cope, you can't do much but cope with the death of a baby, and she would have been spared so much pain and difficulty and anguish. But I knew Lucy would never think that, she loved being alive, she got a lot of pleasure out of the world in all sorts of simple ways. All sorts of complex ones too. I recalled seeing a program on the television in which philosopher Peter Singer said it would be kinder if we did not let badly damaged babies live, and a number of seriously damaged adults made angry responses to that. There was a tiny woman in a wheelchair who had all sorts of problems but had done a great many things in her life, she was wonderful, and in a great fury at the thought that anybody might have taken that away from her. It was her life, she wanted it, she had fought very hard for it and she would continue to do so. I decided that I must not regret that we had put Lucy through a lot in keeping her alive.

And not to mention, our pleasure. Years later, she in turn looked after us wonderfully. She loved us, and cared for us. She did excellent meals when I had to go away, and in the last year of Graham's illness, 1998, she was the one who woke up in the night. He had a personal alarm that made an awful racket but even so I didn't always hear it upstairs. She always did, and got up to him, and got me. It was because he couldn't breathe, and I would dial 000 and the ambulance would come. Mostly they wouldn't have to take him away, mostly they could sort it out at home. The paramedics were always so kind, so patient, so sweet I would have to say. I always thought they were probably relieved that our problems were not caused by drunken knife fights, but even so I still think their kindness was remarkable.

When Graham was a child, growing up in New Zealand, he had what was called a weak chest. He spent a good part of every winter in bed. I wondered how much of this was owing to bicycling to school in bitter Christchurch weather, probably wearing the school uniform of short flannel trousers. And there were no antibiotics, which would have got him on his feet much faster. It was a chore for his mother who was in her forties when he was born. And it was lucky it didn't make him backward in school work – he got excellent scholarships to high schools and then, after Canterbury University in Christchurch, to King's College, Cambridge. One of the school scholarships was to Christ's College, the most prestigious boys' school in Christchurch, another to St Andrew's, a Presbyterian school much favoured by country people. His mother thought the more modest St Andrew's school would be more suitable for the family, a decision Graham never quite forgave her. He did well at St Andrew's, but would have liked more competition, and less conservatism, the school was very what you would have called Country Party, or these days National Party, in Australia. I was conscious that when he became ill in the 1980s with heart problems and then with cancer both of these centred on that weak chest. You'd say that Lucy had a similar focus, and now I wonder if my granddaughter might be somewhat similarly susceptible; you have to be careful when she gets a cold that it doesn't turn into pneumonia, even though she is such a sturdy, healthy little girl. Problem is, day-care centres are hotbeds of childish infections. And as James says, they get a little baby cold and bring it home and give you a full-sized adult dose. The sins of the fathers or anyway the problems of the fathers cast long shadows.

Of course Lucy's trouble was a serious heart defect, not infections, though they often came to be involved. Doctors could never tell us how the heart disease came about, just one of those things, though they did say it would have happened very early in gestation and it would not have been anything that I did, nor could I have done anything to prevent it. I did believe them, but that didn't stop me having feelings of guilt, that somehow it was in some way my fault. Lucy would never have suggested that.

And of course there was not the technology of the present day. No ultrasounds, no checking of heart, brain, lungs, spine, no constant monitoring. Before my grandson was born in November 2016, he had been observed in every detail, there are photographs of every stage of his development. His mother who was having problems with blood pressure was monitored every few hours, bloods and scans taken constantly. The staff kept getting ready to bring him into the world, but decided they could wait a bit longer, until the decision was made. So it wouldn't have been an emergency.

But such things as a child's health do have a dramatic effect on one's life. Overall, and in odd details. Once, it would have been early 1972, when Lucy was five, James just two, we sailed back from Europe in *Canberra*, not nearly as elegant a ship as *Oriana*. We had written to Melbourne's Royal Children's Hospital and arranged to call in for one of her regular check-ups, feeling pleased that we would be able to cut out one long drive to and from Canberra. But when the ship stopped in Melbourne there was a dock strike so it had to anchor out in the roads. People would have to go ashore in shuttles. Then it was announced that the weather was a bit rough and only people disembarking could do this. We explained – could it have been to the captain? Somebody important anyway – about the doctor's appointment, and were allowed to go. When we came back, I remember it was quite late and rather dark, the shuttle had trouble connecting with the ship, it got itself side-on to rather large waves and was nearly scuppered. It was very frightening. Graham couldn't swim and neither could Lucy or James; how could I save everybody if our small craft foundered? But eventually, maybe half an hour later, while we tossed about like a paper boat and water crashed over us, and sailors spoke in hard loud emergency voices, they got it moored to the low landing platform and we partly jumped, partly were heaved, aboard, glad to be safe. The visit to the doctor was quite routine, he was pleased with her, she was okay, strange but okay. It would be another four years and more before she went into heart failure.

Over the years we made a lot of trips to and from Melbourne. Some 800 kilometres the journey is from Canberra, a long way with small children. Once we went when Lucy was about four and James a baby. She was very anxious, much worse than are-we-there-yet syndrome. She was convinced we wouldn't have anywhere to live when we got there. She worried about this all the way. Even when I got a bit cross, and said, Lucy, of course we have got somewhere to stay, would we make you sleep under a bush? But when Lucy had got hold of something to worry about she did not easily give it up.

We'd reserved an apartment at I think the Princes Park motel, which wasn't far from the city. We had a sitting room, two bedrooms and a kitchen, so we could do our own food. Lucy came in the door and looked around her in wonder. Oh, she said, we *have* got somewhere to stay. And it's even got a tree on the wall!

This was one of those murals, really very kitsch, a life-size tree over the whole wall. Lucy loved it. And it became one of those family quotations; whenever people were full of doubts we'd say, And it might even have a tree on the wall.

And I think I did not resist saying, See, we told you so. You needn't have doubted, need you. And she smiled very sweetly at us.

That trip was made in our Renault Eight, which we were very fond of. The same car we drove Lucy home from Melbourne in when she was a few weeks old, with a box in the back of bottles of formula, narrow-necked bottles with small paper bags over them to keep them sterile. Nobody seemed bothered by the bottles spending all day in a hot car. I made use of those bottles, not for me the fancy wide-necked ones with teats that you could turn inside out, I always used the old-fashioned narrow necks. We travelled with a big lidded plastic box and a vat of Milton for sterilising them.

We got back to Canberra just after my birthday. There's a photograph, me sitting in a chair holding this tiny doll of a child in my lap.

After the first operation when Lucy was nine, we drove home in the Peugeot 504; we'd bought it in France, sending an urgent letter to my father to borrow the money. It was comfortable but not air-conditioned and this trip was in the middle of summer, hellishly hot. We stopped overnight at my beautiful sister Brenda and Fred's house in Wagga. They were away, we knew this. It had been shut up for some weeks and was even hotter than outside, and stuffy. It was a nightmare. We opened doors and windows, but Wagga doesn't cool down much at night.

MILESTONES

A wedding

My sister Rosie got married in the spring of 1969. To Athol, an economist. We all went up to Newcastle, we stayed with my parents and Brenda and Fred stayed with his. We went a day or so early and Fred and Graham set off for the Hunter Valley to taste and buy some wine. They went in Fred's Jaguar XK120, a classic shiny black sports car with a long bonnet and a canvas top that was almost never put up. There's a photograph, Fred in proper gear with a cap, Graham wearing a beanie, which gave him rather a thuggish air. He had a luxuriant moustache at that time, which didn't help. They made a sinister couple.

On the way up to Pokolbin the radiator boiled. It was an old car. Fred was wearing leather gloves lined with fur so he thought it would be all right to unscrew it, but the steam shot up his sleeve and then down again inside his glove, getting trapped there and burning him badly. They found a doctor and had it dressed, gave up the idea of wine-tasting and went to some country pub. They asked, Could they have some red wine? Ooh, said the publican, we've got some somewhere, but, I dunno …

He disappeared, came back with a dusty bottle. It's pretty old, he said. I dunno whether it'll be any good anymore.

Their sharp eyes had seen the label. We'll risk it, they said.

I won't charge you much, he said.

It was Penfold's Grange. And wherever it had been, it had aged very happily in that old pub. They asked, Did he have any more, but they weren't so excessively lucky as that.

There used to be quite a lot of such stories about. All gone now, along with unrecognised bottles of Grange.

I talked to my brother-in-law about this narrative and he says I haven't got it quite right. It was an RSL club they went to, and the wine was some amazing Premier Grand Cru French wine. But once there was Grange, and I like that story. My sisters used to read things that I had written and say, Marion, did it really happen like that? I don't think it did, one of them would say, I think it happened like this, I think you're wrong. Write your own narratives, I would say, this is mine and I am sticking to it. But I've got the car right, I asked Fred the exact details.

~

There was the wedding, and the usual reception afterwards, of friends and relations, all the aunts and uncles. I'd made our clothes: Lucy had a navy-blue voile dress with white daisies on it, with little red centres, white crunchy lace stockings and red shoes. She always looked good in dark colours. I'd had her hair cut short because that was supposed to help it curl, it was like quilting over her head. James had an angel top in pale blue Viyella trimmed with guipure lace, with matching bloomers. I had an outfit of heavy white crepe, with swirls of chocolate brown, not too thick, a short dress top with trousers underneath. We didn't discuss our clothes but there seemed a kind of zeitgeist in them: Brenda bought a pale yellow dress and some matching trousers, and Rosie had a Norma Tullo pantsuit with a long fitted and skirted top in ribbed silk, Ottoman silk you could call it. When her daughters got married, tall slender goddessy girls with long red hair, they wore Collette Dinnigan dresses, long and slim and silky, but borrowed Rosie's wedding jacket to wear on top when the evenings got chilly. It didn't quite fit them, they couldn't do it up.

Rosie had a big floppy hat, and there's a photograph of her holding gorgeous chubby James and him grabbing it, both laughing their heads off. Rosie looks beautiful, with long dark hair, her skin pale olive and her brown eyes enormous; she has the soft-faced smudgy big-eyed look that was fashionable at that time. She was twenty-two. What children we were when we got married. Brenda was twenty-one, I was just twenty-three. Quite old, my relations thought. On the shelf.

After the family reception there was another party, at Brenda and Fred's flat, late. We went back to my parents' house and I fed James, lying on the bed in the dark bedroom, snoozing away with him as we always did, then put the children to bed and we went to the party. It was rather wild, as I remember, and Fred wasn't at all well, being a bit delirious with his burnt hand. Brenda made him go to bed, he was sick enough to do what he was told, and Graham eventually threw everybody out. Fred would never have done that, his hospitality was indefatigable, but Graham could, and it was a good idea, some of the people there were heedless and feckless and didn't care about anything when they were drunk and stoned. I was impressed with Graham making people do this, simply by telling them firmly. I was afraid they might have punched him. Rosie and Athol always had a leaning towards counter-cultures. When they moved to twenty acres at Cedar Creek outside Brisbane they had hippies living in the hut at the bottom of the drive, who went on to run a kind of cafe in a cowshed down the road. The hippies were gentle good people. At one stage Athol stopped being a university lecturer and decided to grow avocados and keep poddy calves, but the calves got out and ate the small avocado trees, so it was an expensive and unprofitable exercise. Eventually he went back to being an economics professor.

I sometimes think how grand it was, being the mother of my two beautiful children. I was somehow invincible, nothing could touch me, I was a supremely favoured being. It's funny to look back on that. It doesn't last, of course. Children grow up, and though they remain beautiful they become their own people, they are not yours in that same magnificent way. Bianca is still in that state, just having had her sixth birthday (this was 2014), a beautiful golden child whose radiance illuminates parents and grandparents when they go about with her, but this will come to an end, she will not always so carelessly bestow her beauty on everyone around her.

I remember going to an art exhibition in Berrima when Lucy was, I suppose, about two. She was wearing a dress her granny had made her, cream Viyella with tiny dark pink roses on it, and tights and strappy shoes. By this time, her hair was quite long and honey-coloured. Her granny was famous for her complexion, and so should Lucy have been, and Bianca too, pink and white and glowing smooth – none so fair as they. She was standing against a wall when a woman came gushing up. Joshua Reynolds, she said. Perfect Joshua Reynolds! Lucy squinted up at her, frowning. She didn't know why this strange woman was saying incomprehensible things. Strangers think they can lay claim to beautiful children; Lucy's glowering face told this woman that she couldn't.

We are seven | c. 2006

We had lunch at this time, with some people who were keen to meet us, at Canberra's Little Brussels Cafe, which had Belgian beers, and mussels, and chips. It was new so Lucy never knew it. She loved mussels. Though not beer, she'd have had wine. Or in her last days fizzy water. The cafe was fun because the different beers came in particular glasses, as they do in France. I had a fat goblet of Abbaye de Leffe Blonde. There are pictures on the laminated menu of the glasses the beers come in and I am sure this is how a lot of people choose.

There are descriptions of the beers but it is the pictures of the glasses that charm.

The woman asked me how many children I had. I said one. It was the first time anybody had asked me that question since Lucy died. As I said it my voice faltered, and the woman looked surprised.

I knew it was the wrong answer. I don't have one child. I have two. I did have, I do have. I wanted to cry. I thought that I had betrayed Lucy.

I remember reading Wordsworth's poem 'We Are Seven' when I was at university, and how we mocked it. So sentimental, we thought. The narrator of the poem meets a little girl of about eight, whose beauty makes him glad. He asks her how many sisters and brothers she has. We are seven, she says. But then he discovers that two lie in the churchyard, twelve steps from her cottage door, and that she plays on their graves. Then you are only five, he says. No, she insists, we are seven. Two in the churchyard, two at sea, and the three playing here. However much he insists, she reiterates, 'O Master! we are seven.' He argues:

> But they are dead; those two are dead!
> Their spirits are in heaven!

But the little maid just looks at him, and says, 'Nay, we are seven!'

When I read the poem at university I was as stubborn and stupid as the narrator, and thought it rather silly. But for a while now I have understood the poem to tell a deep truth. The child is right. As far as she is concerned her dead brother and sister are still her siblings, they are still a part of the family, like the two brothers who have gone to sea.

And I, when I said, One, to the woman in the Belgian cafe, had forgotten that, and upset myself. When anybody asks me how many children I have, I will always say, Two. One may be dead, but she is still my child.

And so I have done, since, when people ask me. It's difficult, because then they want to know where she is, what she's doing. Often I want to lie, but I can't. I have to explain that she is dead, and then they catch their breath, and are appalled that they have brought it up. But I like to talk about her.

Later.

Well, such was my resolve. But I cannot always manage it. Because of this business of people asking me, What are they doing? And I find myself having to tell perfect strangers that I happen to be sitting next to at dinner that well, actually one of them is dead. And then I get tears in my eyes and everything becomes emotional.

If I can, I just answer about James, and go on about my granddaughter, which is very easy for me, and with a bit of luck people don't press me. Or perhaps they think that maybe I don't get on with her and don't want to talk about her. It's amazing how many people have a child or two that they are completely estranged from. I want to say, Imagine if your child was dead, what would you feel then? I want to rail at them for their carelessness and stupidity. But I don't. I am quite calm, these days.

Walking | 1967

At one time I thought Lucy would never learn to walk.

This was not because she was not well, or not strong, but because she went on for such a long time simply not walking. She didn't ever crawl either. She sat on her bottom and used her foot, the right one I think it was, to row herself around the floor. She managed this with quite some speed and finesse. I think the polished wooden floors helped, she slid over them easily. But carpets didn't faze her at all.

She was upright, not staring at the floor as she would have been had she been crawling, which is such a boring view, and I think it was this ease and speed that made her not worry about walking. Whereas crawling gives you such a dull view of the world that you can't wait to get upright. And it's hard on the knees, where a nappy-padded bottom is quite luxurious.

I was beginning to envisage her rowing herself to school on her bottom. She could stand up, she would pull herself up on the furniture, but whenever we tried to do that tricky parental thing of holding out a hand to her so that she could take it and walk, then pulling the hand gradually back so that several steps were taken, she gave us a wised-up look and immediately sat down. We could not trick her into it. She could take a step or two if you held her hands but she wasn't interested.

One day, when she was eighteen months old, we were in the bathroom. She pulled herself up against the edge of the bath. I was sitting on a chair. I held out both hands so she could take them and walk to me. But she brushed them aside and walked out of the room. Perfectly. No stumbling, no wobbling, as though she had been doing it all her life.

That afternoon Wendy next door had a birthday party and Lucy walked out, down the steps, across the drive, up the steps, carrying her present. I offered to hold her hand but she didn't need it. Vella, Wendy's mother, was thrilled; she knew about my despair over Lucy's walking. I didn't ring up Graham and tell him. In the evening, when he came home, Lucy ran to the door to meet him. What hugs we had.

James walked at an early age. He got bored with crawling and at about nine months old pulled himself up and practised getting around on two feet. He fell over a great deal, but always pushed or pulled himself up and persevered. All through his toddlerhood he was always falling over, he considered it was part of normal life. Lucy never fell over. The moment she took her first steps she walked perfectly. I realised she had been waiting for that moment. She recognised it when it came and off she went. She didn't like not doing things well. I should never have worried about her. At eighteen months James had been walking half his life. But he did not do it so superbly well as Lucy with her first steps.

~

Bianca did not walk specially early but in her second year she has that mad intrepid quality of her father's and runs around not looking where she is going. She chooses her path and makes for it, not worrying about what is in the way. She walks over feet, toys, books, cushions she has thrown off the chairs, and mostly her gait resembles that of a drunken sailor. She often stumbles, falls over, hits her head, but unless she is tired or in some way feeling fragile she doesn't mind any of this, picks herself up and keeps going. She runs whenever she can. She loves being chased and caught.

Now that she is six she goes to gymnastics classes, since any time she sees a rail or a balustrade or a bicycle stand she does monkey bars on it. She taught herself to stand on her hands by practising every waking moment. In her company you are more often presented with her feet than her face. And when her friend Audrey had her sixth birthday party it was at the rock climbing place: I went up really high Granny, and then there was another one you had to climb up and slide across, and slide across, and slide across, then they lowered you down. I told her about climbing the cliff at Merewether when I was little, a sandstone cliff and almost vertical. Just as well my mother didn't know, I said. How did you get down, Bianca asked. The way I went up, I said.

PRETTY COMFORTS

Cally

Cally and Lucy had been friends all their schooldays and although they went different ways after that they never quite lost touch with one another. One day Cally rang up and said she was working in a dress shop called Pink Ink and why didn't we come in and have a look, it was having a sale and she was sure we would find some interesting things.

We went, and we did. It turned out to be a fabulous shop and pretty soon we were buying all our clothes there. If I were doing some gig for which I needed something new to wear I'd go in, and there would be always something. Lucy used to do work for me, and wouldn't let me pay her, so I used to buy her things instead. The sales were spectacular, and we got a lot of clothes on those occasions. But also I liked to buy things not at sales sometimes, it seemed only fair. And on occasions the owner Jane would ring up and say, I've got just the thing for you, and she was mostly right. She'd bring clothes out, and I'd try them on, and usually they were terrific. Sometimes she'd say, Oh no, take that off quickly, it's no good at all, and she'd be right there too.

Jane herself is a generous woman, in nature and in figure; she wears her own clothes of course and always looks wonderful. She has young women working for her who are impossibly slender; you regard them as beings from another planet who cannot conceivably have anything to do with you. And many of the clothes, at a cursory glance over the racks, look as though they are made for eight-year-olds. But you quickly learn there is no need to be afraid, the girls are very sweet to the no longer young or slender and find amazing things in your size. It's quite a tiny shop but there are always fine things that will fit you, and suit you. And Jane showing you how good a not-skinny person can look.

On special sale days she serves champagne and cupcakes.

I never go shopping to other dress shops. I don't have to put up with bored or supercilious shop assistants, or people telling me I look good when I reckon I look a fright. I go to Pink Ink and it's comfortable and easy and good fun. Sometimes I take my granddaughter in to visit. She loves clothes. At the moment most of her glamorous garments come from the baby market for miniscule sums of money, but one day, perhaps …

At what she calls school but is actually day care (very good and fabulously expensive) there lives a bear called Bernard and the children take him home for weekends. The idea is he will have adventures and be photographed and there will be an album of his doings. Bianca took Bernard to Pink Ink and photographed him among various gorgeous accessories, then to a cafe called Debacle, where he ate pumpkin and fetta pizza and drank a glass of water for lunch, and then to the park where he sat on top of a rock she had climbed. A good time was had by all.

When my sister's son was getting married in Ireland, Brenda came to Canberra to look for a dress. The first thing she tried on at Pink Ink looked fabulous. It was very dear; Brenda demurred. She went back to Wagga, searched there, went to Albury. Came again to Canberra and we went to seventeen shops. By the last I sat on a seat in a state of exhaustion and said, Call me if you want an opinion. Then we went back to Pink Ink and bought that first dress. It turned out to be a bargain. It has seen I don't know how many weddings and glamorous occasions since. The thing is my sister Brenda is famously clever and looks a million dollars on hardly any money; she goes to a designer second-hand shop (with its discards from rich graziers' wives) and to spectacular sales and looks amazing on much less money than I spend on clothes. Of course she is beautiful as well, which helps. I remember at her wedding, she looked glorious, in a plain heavy satin dress. She went on the morning of the day and had her hair done. She hated it, came home and washed it and I fiddled with it a bit and she looked stunning.

Cally doesn't work at Pink Ink anymore but I often have a talk to Jane about how she is going. I realise Cally's daughter Lucy is in high school now; how the years have passed.

Cally was very upset when my Lucy died, she found it very hard to accept. She said she wanted to say something at the funeral. She was very tearful, but very brave too, performing as she wasn't at all used to, and made the kind of speech that is immensely moving because it comes from the heart that is not in the habit of such things.

She said that she had met Lucy on the first day of school. It was recess time and Lucy was sitting on the steps crying. Cally went up to her and asked her why. Because I haven't got a friend, said Lucy. I'll be your friend, said Cally, and she was. She lived just up the street, they went to school together, played, looked after one another. I did not know anything about that first day, and Lucy crying, she didn't tell me, I suppose because it had a happy outcome, or maybe she didn't want me to know about the unhappiness. I did not find out until that day of the funeral. Afterwards I asked Cally why she had gone up to Lucy sitting crying on the steps. Because she was so pretty, said Cally.

At that time Cally – her name is short for Carolyn – was again living nearby and used to come and see me occasionally. She'd knock on the door and say, This time I'm not going to cry. Then she would burst into tears. Even though she had not seen a lot of Lucy in recent years, she found her death very difficult. I was always pleased to see her, and I would cry too.

I am still grateful for that picture of Lucy on her first day of school, my anxious little daughter and dear Cally comforting her.

And now. Cally has died. A cancer. Jane used to give me bulletins. We were optimistic. And then in the middle of 2019 we went to her funeral. At the church of All Saints, which was brought from Sydney stone by stone, gothic arch by patterned window. It used to be the railway station for Rookwood cemetery, in the days when people went to burials by train.

Dear Cally. Not as young as Lucy, but far too soon.

INTERVENTIONS

First operation

We were at the circus when we realised Lucy was ill. It was a children's circus, from Spain I think, I forget its name – it made a speciality of having no animals at all. We sat on tiered plank seats, very uncomfortable, but the children performing were so clever you were supposed not to notice this. I became aware that Lucy was unhappy, not feeling well at all, pale, listless, no energy or enthusiasm. There's a photo I can't bear to look at, showing all these things, as she stands, dogged and puzzled, staring at the camera.

The doctor said she had gone into heart failure, a fairly slow decline, where the heart can't pump blood well enough around the body, and made arrangements for us to fly to Melbourne to the children's hospital immediately. I remember going to see the headmistress of the school where I was teaching, Of course, she said, go. Take as long as you need. It would have been leave without pay, as I was part-time, but the job was kept for me.

For a while we stayed in a motel, and then a friend arranged for us to have an apartment that belonged to the University of Melbourne, used for visiting academics. It was in a 1930s block in Parkville, the hospital suburb, and well set-up for temporary visitors. Lucy's condition was stabilised, but they were not ready to operate immediately; she had an infection in her chest and they needed that to be clear. It was there that we came across the coldness of surgeons for the first time, the brilliance of Mr Clark but his refusal to know us, his detachment, which I did learn to understand. Many of the children he operated on were so badly damaged, had so little chance of survival, he could not allow himself to see them as personalities or he could not do what he did. There were amazing cases of survival but still he had to see them as objects on which to deploy his skill. He was kind and courteous, but remote.

Graham travelled to and from Melbourne, it was the end of the academic year, he could not be away from his job for too long. James went to school, at Errol Street in North Melbourne; it was a famously lively and interesting school, partly poor children, partly children of doctors and such from roundabout. The area had started to gentrify, but plenty of it was original. He had a good time there. He was six, Lucy was nine.

I spent all day at the hospital. Lucy was in a ward of four beds and it was quite sociable. She wasn't feeling too bad, apart from the boredom and panic of waiting. And she was very beautiful, with her long honey-coloured hair and her fine rosy skin. She often wore a nightgown and matching coat, a brunch coat it was called, that I had bought very cheaply from a classy children's shop. It was made of the softest cotton and had stylised roses in tight lines in a dark cyclamen colour with black leaves. Sounds odd doesn't it, and I think a lot of people had thought so, which was why it was so much reduced. It was long with a ruched bodice and frills round the coat and she looked lovely in it, elegant and ethereal. I didn't often dress Lucy in pale pinks and blues, she looked best in odd dark sophisticated colours, because I think her own colouring was so very pretty. She wandered about the ward at will. One day she came back into the room where I was sitting by her bed and spoke in a broken babble of nonsense. Lucy, I said crossly, talk properly, then realised she couldn't, that she was collapsing, her eyes rolling. I caught her, and yelled to the mother opposite to get the nurse, who came instantly and got her to the treatment room. Doctors came.

They said it was a pulmonary embolism. A bit of gunk had come off her failing heart and been pumped through into her brain.

They didn't know what it might mean. I was supposed to go and have dinner with Nancy, whose husband had organised the flat, and her family that night and I rang her up and said I couldn't. Lucy was not exactly unconscious but was mostly sleepy or anyway out of it. We just had to wait and see, doctors said. She now had electroencephalograms as well as electrocardiograms. We watched her, sharp-eyed, trying to see what damage might have occurred. My aunt sent some money to buy her a present and we got a game of Scrabble, and when she was more awake set trembling to play. She seemed okay. But we never knew what harm might have been done. The operation was postponed again.

The Anglican chaplain would come and see her and talk to us, after all she was an Anglican, she had been christened in those first grim days after her birth. He would look at her in a heartbroken kind of way, he wanted to comfort her, and us, but couldn't work out how to. He couldn't talk to her about death but that was clearly what he was thinking about. It seemed often as though we were cheering him up. Everybody in the ward wanted to make Lucy happy. The nurses found a funny little old black and white television set and put it on a table beside her bed, it was the only one in the place. We were watching it on 11 November 1975. It became apparent that something was happening. All the young registrars came and crowded round the bed, avid for news. I remember we didn't think that what was happening possibly could; all of us, the young doctors included, thought that Prime Minister Gough Whitlam would be all right, we all wanted him to be. But he wasn't, the Dismissal happened, the Governor-General claiming to speak for the Queen in getting rid of an elected government, and that time of wonderful vision came to an end. How did we go from such vision to this, how we are now?

Along Flemington Road, which ran past the hospital, there were billboards with rather a lot of white on them that got wonderfully graffitied, with puns on Mal-eficent Fraser and cur/Kerr. James came home from school and asked were we on Gough's side or Malcolm's. Gough's we said, to be sure. Whew, he said. That was the right thing. It would have been bad the other way round.

Now, of course, the 'evil' Malcolm Fraser is seen to be a person of compassion and thoughtfulness and he and Whitlam became good colleagues. Not then. And Kerr who performed the evil deed was never rehabilitated. As Gough said on the steps of Parliament House, addressing with noble heartbreak the people he should have still been governing, Well may we say God save the Queen, for nothing will save the Governor-General. And it turned out to be true. Kerr was falling-over drunk in top hat and tails at, was it the Melbourne Cup? Some such thing. He made himself eminently mockable. He was never able to restore his dignity or reputation.

The day of Lucy's operation came. It would start at eight, nothing would be known before two. We came home and cleaned the flat, oh how it sparkled. Went back before two, sat in one of those anonymous waiting rooms, picked up magazines, put them down, impossible to make sense of words on a page. Again that boredom and panic that you'd think might cancel each other out but have the opposite effect; they carve into one another in a terrible tense hollowness so that physically you don't know what to do with yourself, you can't sit or stand or find any relief. Finally, it was after four, the doctor came. Yes, he was happy, it had worked. They had replaced her missing valve with a tanned pig's valve and sewed up some of the congenital holes in her heart, not time for quite all.

When we saw her she was attached to four different machines pumping drugs into her. Her body temperature was chilled and she had, they explained, been given a controlled dose of curare to somehow paralyse her, so she would feel no pain. But she was alive, doing okay. Later Rosie rang up, and said how shattered she had been when she called and was told Lucy's condition was serious but stable. But she got better and better.

It was close to Christmas. Santa Claus came on a fire engine across the park at the back and climbed into the hospital on the extension ladder, with bags of presents. All the kids who could watched from the windows. Lucy looked peaky and sad; she had to spend time sitting in front of an enormous mirror on a stand, bare to the waist, and watch herself doing breathing exercises. It seemed cruel, to make her look at her perfect little body botched and scarred and lumpily sewn up.

I look at photographs of that time, of the Christmas party in the ward, and they break my heart. She looks haunted, pale, wan, as though she has seen things too terrible to bear. I wonder if maybe that was an effect of the heart-lung machine. Nobody said anything at the time but in the nineties when Graham had his heart surgery we talked to the perfusionist, the specialist doctor who runs the heart-lung machine. The patient's own heart and lungs are bypassed and oxygen-enriched blood is pumped round her body and through her brain by this intricate mechanism. He told us people often have very strange dreams. He asked us to remember Graham's for him, he was writing a book about them. I wonder if Lucy's haunted look is to do with the deep terror of difficult dreams, but we never did talk about it at the time, because we didn't know that such things could come about. One thing she knew was that after the operation her memory was very bad, as though a lot of her life before the heart-lung machine had been erased.

She was allowed to leave hospital and come and stay with us in the flat, but not to leave Melbourne yet. Christmas day, a couple of the young doctors who lived in the hospital-owned Parkville terraces that had a broad green lawn between their backs invited us to come to a Christmas party. They were about our age and had children too. It was three weeks since the operation. One of the kids had a bike and taught Lucy to ride it. I was horrified, I looked at the doctor who was watching, he had been one of the assistants at the surgery; he nodded and smiled and looked pleased. If she is happy, let her do it, he said. So of course we did. By this time she was looking rosy and cheerful, and the haunted look had mostly gone.

Second operation

She had her next operation at the children's hospital when she was twenty-one. This was a difficult decision, and not ours; finally the doctors decided that pediatric surgeons would have a better idea of how to proceed than those who were used to hearts going wrong in later life. Lucy was something of a pioneer of her condition; before her birth children mostly died. Now there is a whole field of congenital heart medicine for adults. Lucy dealt with it all by getting on with what she wanted to do, with what she was interested in, and she didn't think much of these things. She chose not to think of these things.

She was admitted into a ward of cystic fibrosis patients, many of whom were in their late teens or early twenties. They were a jolly lot, frenzied even. They regularly spent periods of time in hospital, attached to drips, and made a mad time of it with their friends. They zoomed around the corridors having races with their drip stands, which were highly decorated with creatures, talismans, charms. While Lucy was there they went on an excursion to the Melbourne show and came back with mobs of stuffed animals, mostly huge – teddies and a red plush devil and larger-than-life puppies. The red plush devil got hidden a lot, the girl who owned him spent a lot of time screaming round the ward hunting for it. They were supposed to keep their strength up and had a kitchen where they could make themselves food day and night, usually toasted sandwiches. They were a cuddly lot and hugged the nurses all the time. Their prognoses were not good, most of them would not live long into their twenties. Whereas Lucy had a better chance of survival. As the surgeon, another of those detached brilliant men, said to her, You've got a 95 per cent chance of getting through this. Of course in your case it will be 100 per cent or nothing, won't it. We looked at pictures of him on the wall sailing in his large yacht and thought, he didn't need to add that.

The week before Lucy's operation he had made front-page news by operating on a day-old baby who had been born with his heart on the outside of his body. He didn't survive, but he wouldn't have anyway, and there was a faint chance that it might have worked. Mainly it was an opportunity for the doctor to see what might be done. A kind of practice, you could say. This case hopeless, but later ones maybe not.

Another day-long operation and terrible waiting. This time we were staying in Ronald McDonald House, and a very strange adventure that was. It was a charity set up by McDonald's in some beautiful old terrace houses, beside the hospital, linked together. One little boy whose brother was in hospital spent a lot of time whining, When was Ronald McDonald coming? He constantly expected him to be turning up with hamburgers. A Chinese woman cooked delicious dumplings, and once gave us some. A diligent reader of my short fiction will find all sorts of little stories from that time. One of the things I noticed was how tattooed many of the young fathers were, and I was conscious how different these tidy artistic scars were from the lumpy bulgy large-stitched jobs of the surgeons. Again we waited all day.

Finally some doctors came and told us, yes, they thought the operation had been a success. Early days, of course. But there was one thing. Something had gone funny with the heart-lung machine, and some bubbles had got in. As soon as they noticed they had reversed it, they hoped none had got into her brain.

And if they had?

Well. Pause. She will be a vegetable.

I suppose you need the truth. But sometimes it's nice if the truth is good news.

We couldn't help thinking it might be a case of the operation was a success, but the patient died.

She was still out to it. We sat beside her. Time passed. It was evening. Late evening. She was lying on a slab of a bed with cot sides, draped in a myriad of tubes, wires, drains. We watched her, holding her hands. Our beautiful bright daughter, who loved words and jokes and poems, stories and plays and puns – how could we live if all that was lost and she was just a lump? Terror was a rock in our chests. Our ears and necks and shoulders ached with the weight of it.

Lucy's eyelashes fluttered, her eyes briefly saw ours. Her lips moved. Hello goobers, she said, sighed and went back to sleep.

I don't know why she called us goobers. It was one of her funny words she picked up somewhere. But when she said it, we knew she was all right. Her self was still there. We walked home to Ronald McDonald House, through the lounge where some young parents sat, staring at the television. We knew they were going to have to decide the next day when to turn their little daughter's life support system off. I stumbled up the stairs, crying for my good luck.

It occurred to me as I was writing this that I could look up the word goober, I might find a meaning. So I googled it: it's a term of endearment really, so Google says. It comes from the ancient Scottish verb 'to goub', which has to do with doing a dance and smiling sheepishly while doing so, exposing the goubs in one's teeth.

I never knew that. But term of endearment it certainly was.

More hospitals, more tests

There were many visits to hospitals, drear, painful, terrifying. The time she was in Calvary, in Canberra, very ill; it was always her lungs that troubled her, and nobody seemed to be able to do anything to help her. The counsellor, Margaret, who had become a friend came to visit her. She knew there were no comforting words that wouldn't be a lie: saying that she was all right, that she would be better soon. It couldn't be done, nobody could know that. That was when Margaret gave her the seashell, in a small box, wrapped in cotton wool, and said, Take this out and hold it when you feel bad, it will comfort you.

It did. Lucy loved that shell, it was a good talisman.

On another occasion we went to Melbourne to an outpatients clinic for people with congenital heart disorders. We stayed at the Windsor. I had been put up there on various official occasions and was on a list for a discount; I would ring up and tell them this was the case and they would say, Of course madame, and so it wasn't too expensive. Lucy enjoyed the porters and the concierge and the pretty bedroom. Our dear friend and beloved colleague Carmel Bird came in and we had dinner, she brought a bunch of roses, exquisite, long ivory-coloured buds furled with dusky pink, in a small round posy. We hoped we were staying only one night so we checked out next morning and left our luggage, but we couldn't leave the roses. So we took them with us. Lucy arrived for her tests carrying this perfectly beautiful posy of roses. Sometimes I carried them, but she always took them back; they were a kind of talisman too. They marked her out as an interesting person, those roses.

One of the tests involved taking arterial blood from her wrist. This is particularly painful and very difficult to do, much much harder than the usual blood-taking. It's often botched, the blood-taker poking about and having to have lots of goes and not making them work, the whole thing excruciating at the best of times. Lucy was normally very brave about having bloods done, but not arterial; she asked for a pain-killing injection first, as a previous doctor had advised. On this occasion the doctor, a rather gaunt and dour woman, smiled slightly, shook her head, slid the needle in and had the blood out and done, still very painful but so swift it was bearable. She admired the roses.

A group of doctors then left her sitting half-naked on a trolley while they discussed her condition as though she was a cat. She was a picture of misery but at the same time she shut off; they didn't see her so she wasn't there. We finished quite early and took a taxi back to the Windsor and had a delicious little lunch. The waiter put the roses in the fridge to keep them fresh. We didn't talk about going to the hospital.

Doctors can be unbelievably cruel. Once in Canberra when she was about fourteen, we went to a pinch-faced chilly specialist who said to her, Of course, you know you'll never have children, don't you? In fact she didn't, we'd avoided such conversations. We didn't ever say the words. Thinking there would be time enough later, when medicine might have come up with new possibilities.

We didn't go back to him again.

On one occasion she stayed overnight at a Melbourne hospital to have more tests. She was in a mixed ward of four people with a bathroom down the middle, which was always littered with sticky plasters from electrocardiograms. Perhaps it was clean but it did not seem so. The middle-aged extremely hairy Greek man in the next bed had to have his chest and back shaved. The hair fell on the ground in great clumps and blew around the floor. Lucy's cousins came to visit. Abigail said in fright: A rat! No, it was a rat-sized wodge of black hair wafting under the bed.

Cardiac Ward, Royal Children's Hospital

(I wrote this in 1975. I write differently now. More plainly. But this is how it felt at the time, so I wanted to include it, and I haven't changed it. This is not a story about Lucy; when this was happening I didn't write about her – it didn't seem fair to turn her into fiction. It's about other children, and I have changed their names. Apart from that it is exactly as it happened. And things like cleaning the flat belong to me.)

The surgery of the heart is more intricate than the doctor's skill knows. He, the operator, the brilliant technician, sees the child only as object, refuses all acquaintance. Otherwise he could not survive his death-dealing. The healthy parents' hearts are sick with fear but the surgeon's eyes slide from theirs, refusing the knowledge of it.

Red-haired Peter's skin glows pink between the freckles. How he blooms, rosy only in euphemism. The real word is dusky. It's the blue blood that oughtn't to be in his arteries that causes it; this afternoon's operation may fix it. There's no certainty, but gleams of hope. He's no longer skylarking breathlessly round the ward, he's resting high in bed, buoyant with sodium pentothal; soon they will come to wheel him to the theatre, ready for the surgeon's performance.

In the waiting room the parents of Josephine wait. Hers was the early show. All morning they have cleaned the flat; it is shining, scrubbed spotless by the energy of their fear. At eight o'clock it began, now it is two, the appointed hour for news. They sit and stand and walk and pick up the magazines and turn pages of which they see nothing. Behind their eyeballs a heavy metal shutter of panic has clanged down and no sight can penetrate, but inside images fester. It is after three.

In the ward the parents of Peter are told there will be no operation for him that afternoon. The theatre is still occupied. Perhaps tomorrow. The parents are peeved, they're psyched up and Peter is dosed up. And flooded with relief. Another day will be added to the seven years, eight months and fifteen days he has now precariously clocked up.

The child sleeps. Red hair and dusky skin bloom. The parents watch. At seven o'clock they go to leave.

How is Josephine? they ask the sister, nervously remembering the tiny four-year-old with large eyes and long brown hair who yesterday sat spellbound on Peter's bed while he plucked awkward notes from his new guitar. The parents of these fragile children constantly bring them presents, perhaps promising themselves, if this inanimate and purchasable object can continue to exist, so must you, my child my dearest flesh. Josephine's mother is knitting her a jumper for next winter, pale almond green with flowers growing across the front, in similar affirmation. The dark-haired child will look lovely in it.

The sister's face pinches. She is no surgeon of averted eye and mechanical but not always sufficient genius. She says, Josephine's parents don't have her anymore. Forgetting perhaps that she is talking to grown-ups (though whoever is old enough?) but more like for her own sake, since all are children in the face of death. The parents' hearts leap and fall and shudder and it would seem cannot go on beating but rally and pump harder than before so the blood rushes sick and giddy through all its chambers.

No wonder such intricate and dreadful organs are sometimes irreparable.

Repetition

I see that I do repeat myself here. Especially with regard to the coldness of surgeons. But I can't cut it out. It's such an enormous thing when you are going through it that repetition is one way of dealing with it. I don't mean that I don't understand, or that I disapprove. It's that it's an immense thing, and I can't stop thinking about it. Like the shell, and Bianca having Lucy in her heart. But those are good things, and dealing with surgeons though it might have a happy ending isn't pleasant at the time.

Caravaggio with chips and ice cream

We went to Sydney, to the Transplant Clinic at St Vincent's Hospital, to see if Lucy might be considered a suitable candidate. She was, oh, thirty-seven, thirty-eight. The surgeon was again formal, polite, cold, the usual thing. I've learnt it's because they are conscious that their interventions might kill you, so they don't want to get to know you beforehand. Moreover they know they are probably going to be telling you unpalatable, cruel, mortal truths, and they have to keep their distance.

This woman was slender, power-dressed, much younger than me. She went through all the possibilities. She said that Lucy ought to have a triple transplant – heart, lungs and liver – which had a number of implications. Donor organs would be extremely hard to come by. And a big question was Lucy's state of health. Would she be strong enough to cope with such radical surgery? Fortunately these were questions that could not be decided at this moment, they would need a lot of consideration and further study. So we were allowed to go off, in a state of gloom indeed, but a kind of reprieve; we did not have to make up our minds just yet.

We caught a taxi to the Art Gallery, to the Caravaggio exhibition. But first we could have lunch. We went to the main dining room and sat and looked at that glorious Sydney view of the harbour and the Finger Wharf. Lucy said, Can I order whatever I like? And of course I said, Of course! Anything you like. So she ordered a serve of chips and a bowl of ice cream, with a bloody Mary. If the waiter was at all bemused by this grown woman eating child's food, he did not in any way let on. He brought it with all his waiterly finesse. I recollect that I ordered *vitello tonnato* and a vine-ripened tomato salad, with wine to drink: enough sophistication for the both of us. Lucy sat and ate her chips, voluptuously, with her fingers, one by one. They were very beautiful chips, very thin, very crisp, the best kind, the wickedest kind, which is why they are the best. And when the ice cream came she ate that with slow pleasure and I was so delighted that she was enjoying herself.

Once she would not have ordered ice cream and chips. From a baby she loved food. Going to England on the boat when she was six months old, travelling in England and France and Italy, from an early age she graduated from apple puree and ate what we did with great gusto, at home and in restaurants. She didn't always eat a lot, and when she was small I needed to make sure she was eating enough, but her choices were always sophisticated and interested. With exceptions; she never cared for offal, except for chicken liver pâté, but that's about all I think. She was keen on things like garlic and olives and blue cheese, which are often not thought bland enough for small children. I remember when James was born, she was three, some friends invited her and Graham to lunch and then they came into hospital to see me. Lucy climbed all over the bed and gave me cuddles and kisses and breathed garlic fumes in my face; they'd all been eating home-made pizzas. I remembered being jealous. I don't recollect what I'd had for lunch but it had been dreary hospital food, not this rich sensuous garlic-perfumed reality. That was 1969; not a lot of people cooked real pizza at home in those days.

It was so nice, this little soft-cheeked rosy sweet-scented child climbing all over me breathing powerful garlic in my face.

But in the months before that Art Gallery meal I knew Lucy was gradually going off food. And wine, which she had loved. First of all she stopped drinking white wine, and then wasn't very keen on red, either. She preferred vodka drinks, bloody Marys, or with lime, which had not been at all her taste before. She lost interest in a whole lot of foods she'd enjoyed. She'd been a great cook, and even today when I open many cookbooks there will be lists in her handwriting of dishes she planned to cook, or had already cooked. When I was on the Australia Council for the Arts and frequently travelled interstate for three- or four-day meetings, arriving back late Friday evening, she would have ready some marvellous meal to welcome me home, and the three of us would sit down to a feast. She would have been cooking for Graham while I was away, going through books, trying out new recipes, which she always made work. But I stopped travelling like that, and she gradually stopped cooking, and then she began to stop eating. She'd sit at breakfast swallowing pills and drinking bubbly water and not feel like anything to eat.

And then I realised that one of the most important things in our relationship was being denied me. I had always got great pleasure in feeding people I love, and now this child whom I loved so dearly could not accept what I had to offer. Not would not, could not. I think it frightened her. She did not like to consider it, I am sure wanted to regard it as a passing phase, shortly she would be back to eating with pleasure again. But she was afraid, and so was I. I tried not to let terror be a guest at our meals. She'd often had moments of pain, and delicious food and wine had alleviated that; now I was helpless, I did not know what to do to make her feel better.

So I loved sitting with her, watching her, eating her chips, her ice cream, in the cafe of the Art Gallery of NSW. Such a miserable morning, and now so much pleasure. And then we went and looked at the Caravaggio, me pushing her in a wheelchair so that she didn't get tired. She hated the wheelchair, but accepted its usefulness; I suppose that is how most people feel about them. She was thrilled by the exhibition; she'd majored in fine art at university and knew what she was looking at. We had time to gaze at it all. Afterwards she bought a CD of music of his period which she adored. I still play it. We did wonder if Caravaggio had ever listened to any of it, but who cares when you are playing Palestrina, Monteverdi, Gabrieli. She bought two bell-shaped glasses to give to Rosie for her birthday.

This was in February 2004. We heard little from the transplant clinic, an odd holding letter. Lucy decided she was never going to hospital again, certainly never subjecting herself to the terrors of such invasive surgery. She knew the big one would be horrible.

And then it was that one morning in November of that year, she lay on her bed to have a nap, with her cat curled beside her. She didn't wake up. I think her subconscious gave her permission to escape in this only way she could the all too familiar hi-tech depredations of a heart-lungs-liver transplant. Dying wasn't something she really thought about but her subconscious was ready. Some time later, the clinic sent a final bill that had been forgotten, they said. I considered sending it back, saying, No longer in this world, but I paid it.

~

I have to add to this, that her brother James does not agree with me. His evidence is the meal he cooked for her the night before she died. He and his partner Julee went round because I was unwell and in hospital and made her favourite dish, pasta carbonara, and they got an excellent bottle out of the cellar and had a wonderful feast and were very happy. A lovely thing about Julee was her fondness for Lucy. That night Lucy's reluctance in the face of food wasn't apparent. James is sure she had no thought, conscious or subconscious, of wanting to die. On the contrary, it was her greatest fear, he says. It is a happy thing for him that they had that night together. My husband, John, stayed with me in the hospital till late and then went to the house after Lucy was asleep and spent the night because he did not think she should be alone. In the morning, early, before he went to work he had a brief conversation with her. Lucy said, I'm all right, Mum's all right, everything is all right. Several hours later she curled up and went to sleep and died. I tried to ring her up and got nothing but an engaged signal. James and Julee came to visit me at lunchtime and, alarmed that the phone had been engaged for several hours, went home to see how she was. James says that as soon as he stopped at the house he was discomfited to see the sitting room curtains still drawn; Lucy always opened them to let the sun in. The front door was locked, the house was silent, too quiet. Lucy wasn't sitting in her usual place. They called out; no response. They walked into her room, she was lying on the bed, had been sitting on it and had lain back. With the phone in her hand, in the middle of ringing. The cat on the bed, curled up beside her. Julee says that the sound of James's voice is carved on her memory, calling her name. Lucy! Lucy!

He thought of resuscitation. She was very cool. James says it was the worst moment of his life.

He called 000. What service did he want? It was a dead person, he said. The fire brigade came first, traipsing in with their great padded uniforms. They were pleasant and kind. Attentive. Then the police, then the ambulance. A death alone is a suspicious death. They put Julee and James in separate rooms so they couldn't co-ordinate their narratives, though they had already had plenty of time to do so.

They asked about existing conditions. Oh yes. Medication? Yes again. They said she seemed extremely peaceful, which was good for James, who was worried about that phone in her hand. He had to tell the story three times. What about a doctor? Yes, our lovely GP Denise, who has held our hands through all sorts of times, who came and sat at the kitchen table and drank coffee with us when Graham died in 1998 and just talked, gossiped really. But nobody could find her. Messages were left. Another doctor was called in and said the right useful things. Then Denise came.

Everybody left. The undertaker came. James sat with Lucy. The undertaker said to remove her jewellery because we were unlikely to get it back. Bracelets and rings. There was a ring she never took off. It stuck. James said, Come on Lucy. He pulled, there was a little snap. I'm sorry if I broke your finger.

A number of people telephoned to talk to us; Carmel rang, she'd heard I was ill. James made a lot of calls. First he rang Brenda, Fred answered. He called Rosie. Called work (it was the National Library) to tell them he was not coming back very soon. Everyone he could think of; suddenly the news was spreading out in quick long tentacles. Her friends Leonie and Simone. Going through Lucy's address book. Friend Helen. He couldn't reach her. She called eight years later, she'd been on the run from an abusive husband. Lucy had had a birthday present waiting for her, glamorously wrapped as she always did. But by then it was too late.

I was in hospital with labyrinthitis, caused by a virus apparently. *The Taste of Memory* was newly released and I had been running around doing promotion, and had caught some infection. I was too dizzy to stand up. I had woken up feeling like this, and had gone back to bed, thinking it might pass. We were having our friends from Adelaide, the Susans, Susan Magarey and Susan Sheridan, for dinner. I remember what I was planning to cook: *saumon en papillote*, the fish placed on a piece of foil, with a little chopped onion, some olive oil, dill, a tablespoon of pastis to give a fresh aniseedy flavour. A package for each person. I planned to go to the market in Civic, buy the fish, some green beans, cheese, grapes, and I can't remember what for a first course. But gradually I realised the dizziness was getting worse and I felt very peculiar; I crawled downstairs, hanging on to the banister, got Lucy's blood pressure machine. It was about 240; frightening.

It's usually 130. I thought I might be having a stroke. That's when I called the ambulance; they fiddled around as they do, in that stabilising fashion, and took me to hospital. I sent the Susans an email, hoping they'd get it, but unable to pay any more attention. I gave Lucy a hug. She was calm, said I would be better soon. I suppose she was too calm, I should have been concerned. She would normally be extremely worried, but I was in no state to think of that.

The hospital was very suspicious, muttered about drink and drugs, which was a great shock to me; always when I took Lucy and Graham to hospital people were so sweet, so sympathetic, so kind. But shortly they were like that with me too.

A lot of people who read *The Taste of Memory* told me that it was a book about Lucy; what pleasure it gave them that she so informed it. A lot of them said that in a kind of marvelling way. I hadn't thought of this when I was writing it, but after that I looked at it and they were right. Her presence is there throughout the book, as a companion, as a source of ideas, as a provider of recipes. She's there in its stories. I was pleased that she was so present in the book, especially as it was unconsciously that I had made it happen. These readers, and I as well, see it as a kind of memorial to her. A tribute to her charm, her benign presence, her love for so much.

Some people said they cried when they read it, that Lucy would not be these things again.

James tried to ring me up, but the hospital said no, they couldn't get me; he could leave a message. He didn't think this was stuff for a message. John at work talked to him on the phone, and he said he'd go out and tell me. Now the hospital staff were very friendly. I was still in emergency, but they dressed me in two gowns, one for the back, one for the front, because of the gaps, put me in a wheelchair and took me to a room where bad news is given. As soon as I saw John I somehow knew what this was going to be.

After that they looked after me. Put me in a private room. A nun, a friend of Nancy's, came to visit me (it was Calvary Hospital, still a few nuns volunteering about the place). She gave me a card, and a hug; I cried in her arms. The card said that I should always remember that I had held Lucy's hand as long as I could, and that made me cry too. That idea of holding her hand, for thirty-eight years I had done it, more than half my life, and now I couldn't anymore. Suddenly I got a terribly sore foot, nobody knew what it was, they couldn't make it better. I stayed in hospital as long as I could but finally the deadline for burying her approached; we had the funeral on the last day possible before we needed to embalm her; I couldn't bear that, I wanted her to be left at peace. We dressed her in her favourite clothes, with some beautiful slide-on velvet slippers with turned up toes, which she loved to wear. When I kissed her in her coffin she was cold and waxy, not the soft-skinned rosy girl she had been, alive.

I went to the funeral in a wheelchair. It was gout, they finally decided; I'd never had it before. Probably brought on by stress. It made me powerless to do anything but just sit. But I felt like that anyhow.

~

I was having a rather long correspondence with an old friend, the Joyce scholar Clive Hart, in 2005 and wrote this in a letter to him:

> In fact I feel sad a lot of the time at the moment. I think that when Lucy died I thought of her, and how it was really a good thing for her, that life had got very hard and was only going to get harder. But now that time has passed – it is more than seven months – I am feeling much more selfish and just missing her so much, conscious many times a day what fun, what delight and pleasure there was in having her, her lively mind, her loving heart,

in my life. I tell myself all that about things getting harder for her but it does not do much to counteract my loss.

A last supper

Why do I say supper? We never call it that. In our house we always say dinner. When I was a child at home we called the evening meal tea, but in my youth I listened to the world with sharp ears and knew the right word was dinner and so that was the word I said – I often trained myself into the use of words and syntax I knew to be desirable, like napkin for serviette, sofa for couch, different from instead of to – and so my children were brought up to say dinner too. I read Nancy Mitford and decided that even if I was working class I would speak proper.

Supper was what we had late in the evening after dinner. Sometimes we played the card game 500, visiting my parents in the family house by the sea, warm salty evenings and my father sighing that we weren't watching the cards. That's a boy on a man's errand, he would say. There was a tradition of onion sandwiches and cups of tea: the bread a bit doorstoppy, plenty of butter, the onions doused with vinegar. Not often, those suppers, but in the way a thing done several times seems a long tradition.

But I know why I say supper. Supper has meanings of finality and memory and that is what I want here.

It is Monday. I had failed to go to the shops for the third day in a row, looking in the fridge and making do with what I could find. But tonight it was bare, and I had the idea of going into the freezer. I don't run a good freezer. Egg whites and pots of stock and odd nameless things that I will throw out when I get around to it, certainly nothing I would dare eat, the names worn off and the dates lost in the ice of time. But I know there is a plastic box of Suleiman's pilaff.

I have been making Suleiman's pilaff since the year I was married. An Elizabeth David recipe, from her first book, *Mediterranean Food*. I discovered when I read her biography recently that it is named for her cook in Egypt during the Second World War. It is made of diced roast lamb, fried with tomatoes and onions, garlic, pine nuts, raisins and rice, all cooked in dripping but these days I use olive oil, and served with thick Greek yoghurt. Sometimes I spit-roast a leg of lamb just so I can make Suleiman's pilaff with the leftovers. David describes it as a comforting dish, and our family has always been very fond of it, except James who didn't much like fruit in savoury dishes, though he says that now he does. I'd cooked too much for Lucy and me to eat, and instead of leaving it in the fridge to go stale and be thrown out, I had put it in a small plastic pot, labelled it with felt-tip pen, and frozen it, thinking that one day when I was out it would be just enough for Lucy to eat. It would be Lucy at home and me out and a good little savoury meal for her.

I took it out and put it on the sink to defrost, remembering how delicious it had been, how we had enjoyed eating it.

The date was still decipherable, just: 3.11.04. Not so long ago. Just before Lucy died. I thawed it out and warmed it up, thinking it might be quite nasty but it wasn't, it was delicious. I spooned dollops of yoghurt on it and drank some red wine, and vividly I could recall that the last time we ate this dish, this very dish, not just the same recipe, Lucy and I had been so happy together, eating this marvellous comforting food and watching *The Bill*. Lucy was always such fun to watch crap television with, we'd explode into laughter at the impossible plots and the characterisations that would change according to the needs of these ever more bizarre narratives, enjoying so much our joint perceptions of their silliness. Now I find watching television on my own dreadfully boring.

That is why I call it a last supper; it was the actual food we ate together, and I ate it again in the memory of her.

Next morning. I wake up and after a while getting my thoughts into order realise that today is 10 May. It is six months today since she died. I cannot believe it. Neither can John, or James, or Carmel, when I tell them. It is because she is so much always with us.

Carmel sends me this email:

> Marion, you are so deeply sad that your sorrow transcends its own darkness and is transformed into such a sweet lightness that it informs your being and visits everyone who knows you.

I am not sure that this is true but I am greatly comforted that she should say so. Carmel is so good; she insists that of course I must feel sad and always finds ways of helping it be a good thing.

INVENTORY

Sons of heaven

Lucy was very fond of things, and I was pleased by her pleasure in them because she did not have very much else. She did not have a lover, not later on, or a husband or children, she did not have a job or a busy or varied life, she could not do very much, so things were a comfort and an interest. And of course they were most frequently things for other people. She was a wonderful giver of presents, she thought hard and chose carefully and came up with a host of gifts. And she took an interest in other people's things.

I've often quoted Dr Johnson on this matter: 'Words are the daughters of earth … things are the sons of heaven.'

It's a remark from someone who thinks sons are more important than daughters, but you don't have to agree with this mad notion to like the quotation. I once was going to call a novel *Daughters of Earth* but my agent said people would think it was a book about Soviet Five-Year Plans, which it wasn't at all.

Ugg boots

I used to think ugg boots were quite dreadful objects but seeing a picture of Pamela Anderson wearing them with a bikini gave me pause. Moreover my feet are frail and the house is cold often so I started to covet some ugg boots. Lucy took up the idea and we went to a shop and she bought them for me, long pale brown suede. She didn't want any for herself; she bought some low slippers lined with fleece, to replace Granny's that she had been wearing since 1987; they were quite worn out and shabby, but mainly not warm anymore.

So every time I sit in my study with cosy warm feet in ugg boots I think of Lucy.

PS – On ugg boots: when it is really cold, as in this winter of 2006, or you have got a cold and feel distinctly seedy, warm feet in ugg boots are the most luxurious and lovely thing. And now it is the winter again and I am still wearing these very same boots.

Vogue Living

For several years she had given me a year's subscription for Christmas. Now when I go out to the letterbox and see a new one wrapped in plastic I cry a bit, because there it is, an emblem of Lucy's love. I read it slowly, rationing it. I think after this year when the subscription is finished I shall renew it.

A grape-coloured cardigan

One day Lucy went to Alibi where we often bought wonderful clothes. That was in the days before Pink Ink. They were having a sale and she bought some things for herself then came home and said there was a cardigan which was just right for me, she'd asked the girls to put it away, I had to go and try it on. I did. It was a fine knit, in a soft dim purplish grape colour, quite long, with a collar and a sort of peplum round the bottom of some odd stiffish fabric. I quite liked it, not a lot, but Lucy had been so keen that I bought it. Almost immediately it became one of my favourite garments. It is quite old now and I have found a couple of small holes in it which I have mended; I will be heartbroken when it wears out. I wore it to the doctor the other day.

She said, You are looking very trim. I knew I wasn't any thinner, it was just that the cardigan flatters me. How clever of Lucy to know on simply looking at it that it would suit me so well, please me so well.

Rose cream

A pot of hand cream, fiendishly expensive, I know, from Crabtree & Evelyn. They make a line of unguents perfumed with damask rose, but this one has the scent of a rose called Evelyn, specially bred for its richness. I rubbed it into my hands last night and I can still smell it now as I type, faint, caressing; I have rinsed my hands since but do not want to wash them carefully. Lucy loved scents. I bought them for her, her father used to, she bought them for herself. Sometimes I wear her perfumes; I like that. Dune, Samsara, Byzance. I gave her Cinnabar to Rosie. She always wears that and indeed Lucy bought it for herself because she liked it on Rosie.

Candles

Two candles scented with Fidji, which was the perfume I was wearing at the time. Graham would have bought it for me, he liked to give me French perfume. In fact when we first met he bought me a little array of sample bottles so I could choose the one I liked; at that time it was Antilope, which doesn't seem to exist anymore. I put these candles on a shelf and then somehow forgot to consider them, or I did, from time to time, but it never seemed the right moment. I thought, you can't use scented candles for a meal, it has to be some occasion when they aren't competing with robust savoury smells, and wine.

Yesterday I called the technician to come and look at my stove, and then suddenly looked at the range hood, it was filthy with greasy dust. Not long ago my sister Rosie was staying. She said, I think you need somebody in to spring clean. I thought she was referring to the general level of cleanliness in the house. I do have a cleaning lady, I said. I think you need a thorough scouring out, she said. After that I had my cataract operations, and now I can see what she was talking about.

Anyway, I cleaned the range hood, and the shelves beside it, and took down the candles, wrapped in cellophane, and also rather dirty with greasy dust. I took one upstairs and lit it, lying in bed reading and watching its small steadfast flame burning.

I couldn't smell any Fidji. Hardly even candle wax. Would it have ever given off the odour of the perfume, or was that a bit of a trick? Who knows. I was sad that I had not lit them earlier, so that Lucy could have seen, but then she would have been disappointed with her certainly expensive candles. I looked at the unwavering flame, it is nearly two years now since she died, it's July 2006, but I still think of her all the time. How good to be one of the 90 per cent of American people who believe in heaven (I read that statistic in the paper today); I could imagine her seeing me and knowing that at last I was enjoying her candle.

Spade

I am quite a hard person to buy presents for because I seem to have what I need. I don't think this is a matter that is personal to me, a lot of people have a lot of things and don't particularly need any more. Lucy was very good at working out the spaces where something useful would fit. She bought me a spade, a small stainless steel blade with a polished wooden handle, very beautiful, strong and light to use. I don't dig the garden a lot, it is so full of tree roots that to get into the soil I have to use a mattock, but when I want to dig with a spade, this is such pleasure to use.

Cookbook

One day at a Melbourne Writers Festival I went to the launch of a glossy book by Manuela Darling-Gansser, called *Under the Olive Tree*. She irritated me – she was extremely thin, chic, sharp – and I thought, that's one book I shan't be buying. My birthday came, large book wrapped. Yes, the very one. Lucy said, I knew you were really keen to have it, so I got it. It was expensive, and we didn't often spend money on expensive cookbooks. Of course I said I was thrilled, and I was, that she had bought me a present so thoughtful, even if the thought came from crossed wires. And then I looked at it, and it was not only very beautiful, with pictures by Simon Griffiths of meals being eaten in gorgeous settings that make you want to step into them, but it also had a lot of interesting recipes of the kind I like: simple, tasting good, of themselves. Like the fennel salad: very finely sliced, dressed with the juice of a lemon, olive oil and some capers. Brilliant with flathead tails simply cooked in olive oil. Every now and then I look at it, and cook something, and remember the pleasure she got from giving it to me, and each time I enjoy the pleasure of receiving it. A gift of love, as all hers were.

Turtle

Once I was feeling rather out of sorts. I can't remember why. I am lucky, I don't suffer from depression, but this day I felt quite grumpy. Lucy was going shopping, and called at the garden centre and bought me a small bronze turtle. It fits neatly in the palm of my hand. She said that when I felt glum or not happy I should hold it in my hand and I would feel better. I keep it beside my bed and I do pick it up and hold it sometimes, and Lucy was right. I feel good when I hold it. Not because there is anything magic in a turtle, but because it was given with love.

In Vietnam they think a lot of turtles, or is it tortoises? I am not sure I know the difference when it comes to small bronze objects. They believe the world rests on the back of a turtle. When you ask what is underneath the turtle, the answer is, turtles all the way down.

Once, when we lived in Paris, we had two small turtles in a glass box of water and weed. They were called Captain Face and Doll Common, because we had recently been in London and gone to see *The Alchemist*, the Ben Jonson play. It had John Woodvine in it, whom we knew from *Z Cars* (so long ago). The kids loved it. We didn't use the turtles' names much, too much of mouthfuls. Not to mention pretentious.

Ceramic figures

A Bev Hogg strange angel, sideways rectangular, with red boots and wings and tiny paw-like hands. A cat, also winged, gauzy blue pottery wings, with a fierce smile and a sunburst on her head. Gifts from Lucy.

Emails from Lucy

She and Carmel would write often. Emily and Sylvia were Carmel's cats, beautiful Siamese. Raphael was her little dog.

From: Halligan Family
To: Carmel Bird
Date: Wednesday, 3 December 2003 3:03 PM
Subject: Re: to Lucy

Dearest Carmel, Em, Sylv and Raphy,

Are you getting any reasonable walking with your floods????? Sounds very, extremely dreadful. Worst storms in Vic in 100 years. Yikes. Inordinately newsworthy. Much (and needed) rain here ditto, though now sun begins to poke head through as though it might party. Probably just get muggy - er.

Am off to Jim and Jules's apartment ce soir, for meal and DVD. No more videos for them, ho ho. I have asked for, of all things, *The Hulk.* This is demonstrating my huge bad taste.

Heard Milly was almost abandoning you with your buying the Di book at Target. You are SOOOOO cool. Have you read it yet??? [This was a biography of Princess Diana about which Carmel's daughter was very scathing.]

Off to look at piccies that Fred (uncle) sent via email. They are in Ireland, visiting coz Ben and his girlfriend's family.

Thanks for missive,
love and hugs,
Lucyxxxxxxxxxxxxo

John Thompson is a dear friend of ours who used to work at the National Library and is now a freelance curator and writer of books in Sydney. He and Lucy often talked books.

From: Halligan Family
To: John Thompson
Sent: Wednesday, 25 June 2003 9:55 AM
Subject: Re: lite read

Dear John,

Daniel Deronda is no small task! It's a mighty tome isn't it? Though highly readable. Ma was racing with the tv production: some weeks she was ahead, other weeks the programme cut too much across chunks of it, and quite left her reeling.

Getting myself worked up to and sorted travel-wise for this yearly trip to Melbourne to visit my Adult Congenital Cardiac Clinic. Not specifically mine, but I do feel a sense of returning to a familiar stomping ground.

Marion and I have decided to take an extra day, so not zip home, but browse a little, catch up with our Carmel, and Fran Bryson. And perhaps visit the odd shop or gallery, lungs permitting.

Must go downstairs now. Ma has just left for Newcastle, and the kitchen looks a little like a bomb just went off. And I have our cleaning gal coming in about half an hour.

Take care,
love and hugs,
Lucyxxxxxxxxxxxxxo

A letter – from me | 22 June 2005

Dear Lucy,
I have decided to write you a letter, since I seem to spend quite a lot of time talking to you. Why not write it down. I would like to think that you might read it, but I doubt it. Remember Peter French said, when Graham died, that he could see him driving around heaven in his Peugeot visiting vineyards and tasting good wines. Such a lovely image, and how we enjoyed it. We didn't believe it, but we enjoyed it. It had a certain gravitas, coming from your heart doctor and his. Now Kate Llewellyn has said that you have gone from the care of one parent to the other. I love to think of that, and I can think of it, in the way you can hold a thing in your head that could be true, that ought to be true, though you are fairly sure it isn't. You were much firmer in your disbelief

than me. I don't think of any possible afterlife, or continuance of life, as a matter of Peugeots or vineyards or a welcoming parent on the other side, but neither do I quite believe that you have completely ceased to exist, as you and Graham were so firmly certain happens after death.

Smarter people than me have believed in such things, I say to myself, and envy them. That Victorian certitude that a dead child was in the arms of angels and that all the family would be reunited in the next life: how wonderful that would be. The graveyard at Eden is full of such convictions. Some people still have them; John's brother who is a Mormon has a record of all his family and its branches and shoots and roots, so that when the Day of Judgment comes God will know whom to save. I can't imagine God needing a card index to tell him these things. Surely he would have the most up-to-date computer, would be the most up-to-date computer, he is omnipotent and omniscient after all. And though I can be comforted that better minds than mine have believed that death isn't the end of everything, and consider that were this to happen it would be in all sorts of ways we can't comprehend – I once used the image of a mouse in the house, watching me use a computer, talking on the telephone, making coffee, what could a mouse know of such things, it would be entirely uncomprehending; and maybe the universe was full of equally amazing unknowables for humans? I also fear that those better minds just wanted comfort, they wanted to believe that their loved ones and they themselves for that matter would not be forever lost.

Of course you aren't forever lost, not while I still talk to you. Sometimes I tell you nice things, amusing things. More often I think, oh how pleased Lucy would be to hear that, know that, see that. K9 back on *Doctor Who*. The new Doctor Who. The quinces.

James and Julee getting engaged. So many things, every detail of daily life that so amused and entertained you. And quite often, I have to say, I reproach you. That you have gone away and left me, and how am I going to cope on my own?

James said that on the day you died and he came home and found you he walked round the house telling you off. In quite violent terms. Lucy, you tool, was one of the things he said, how could you do this to us? He was so upset that he had to express his anger and misery directly to you. I wonder, did you have any awareness of that? I do think that a person does not die, *cut*, like that. That some consciousness remains, for a little while, perhaps until the body begins to cool, perhaps longer. That the soul as it leaves the body lingers for a while where its life has been. The little medieval manikin of the drawings, rising up from the mouth of the body it inhabited, taking its leave slowly.

And there is a giveaway: I have used the word soul. I do believe we have souls, and if I believe that, surely I must think that they don't die when we do?

Ivonne who is not just our house cleaner anymore has appointed herself to look after me. She inquires do I have smoke alarms (the day after we went next door and watched the Curlies' fireworks, how you would have enjoyed that, sitting on their back deck drinking wine, watching the tiny explosions zooming and fizzing and showering sparks of light, and I'd put a piece of lamb in the oven and came home three quarters of an hour later to find a terrible stench of burning and the house full of smoke; I don't know what I did wrong but the meat under its burnt crust was deliciously pink and tender – probably a bit too pink for you); worries about the hot-water tank leaking; she thinks I need to be taken care of, now you are not here to do it for me. She hopes that you have made contact with her mother in the next world, who died when she was a child, in Colombia, and maybe a message will come. She dreamt about you, that you rang her up, and you said life was very calm and peaceful where you were and it was all going very well. She was deeply moved by this, as though it had really happened. She hopes for a sign, from you and from her mother. She thinks that maybe the dream was one. A sign.

I nearly forgot: I went to see Denise (our GP) the day after the pope died (just routine, prescriptions, blood pressure checks and such) and she said, That pope, I bet he's already met up with Lucy and she's been giving him a piece of her mind. So you see, your reputation.

Sometimes I think you know all this. That when I think, Lucy would have loved that, that maybe you are somewhere, loving it. I can't imagine that wherever it is you would be too ethereal to care about the ordinary things that meant so much to you, even if it is in a cool and remote way.

I still can't program the video recorder, though I can tape programs directly. I had to get Sam next door in when I stopped being able to work your telly; at fourteen he is a bit old for this sort of thing but very good. (I've bought a DVD player, it's very clear – and pretty easy, once James set it up for me.) I've sort of learnt to do the BAS. And I mostly remember to pay the bills. But you should hear me grizzling, more words for Lucy. About you deserting me, leaving me with all these terrible things to do by myself. Of course this is self-pity, I don't suppose you would mind much not having to do these chores. That's the selfish part of me missing you.

And of course I have a lot of conversations with dear old cat Josie about you not being here. She is pretty unimpressed, let me tell you. And she weighs a ton on the bed – remember how

I would never let her sleep with me? Now I don't have the heart to turn her away.

The thing I would really love you to know is all the letters and cards and notes I have got. From all sorts of people, some who only met you once. I know you would be astonished at how much people loved and admired you. You were too modest ever to have any belief in that. But a wonderful number and variety of messages came. People took the trouble not just to send conventional sympathy but to write to tell a story that they had been involved in with you, narratives whose existence I never suspected. They are still coming, more than seven months later. They still make me cry. Alan Gould has put you in a poem, and Kate has dedicated a book to your memory. Alan's poem comes from something that John said at the funeral, about your response to the television.

I have to say, watching telly is so dull without you. That whole evening ritual of the news, and cooking dinner, and the *7.30 Report*, and opening a bottle of wine, and paying attention to what was happening on the box as much as was needful: talking loud when Prime Minister John Howard came on, humming, averting our eyes; laughing our heads off at Downer; berating Beasley for being so feeble, so lacking in vision; cheering Latham on, willing him to remain strong and stroppy, all the things we liked him for at the beginning. I can't do that on my own; I just feel depressed. All I can do is mute the buggers. We always got the balance right, between talking and making fun and having conversations and paying attention when we needed to.

Even watching *Who Wants to Be a Millionaire* was fun with you: interactive television. I can't do it now.

Last night Howard came on and I was about to get rid of him when I realised the host, Kerry O'Brien, was doing a wonderful job on him, about refugees, and Howard was squirming. Kerry was really getting to him. Not that that will have any effect, a few minutes' discomfort then he will go back to rejoicing in his rat cunning. And the ABC did quite a wicked thing, and will no doubt suffer. At 6.30 they had a half-hour interview with Max Gillies, talking about his new show, *The Big Con*, and it included some lengthy footage of his current impersonations of Howard. So good, especially when we had what passes for the real thing an hour later. I thought, how Lucy would have loved this. Some excerpts too from the old days of the *Gillies Report*. Max is much more savage now. I always remember how he kissed you on your sixteenth birthday. We'd gone – all four of us I think – to see him do the one-man show *Scanlan*, and Mrs Donnolly the librarian at Campbell High invited us to a party after the show. Her daughter was stage manager of the play, and you and Mrs Donnolly were good friends because you spent sport and PE periods in the library helping her. Max kissed you for your birthday and you didn't want ever to wash your cheek again.

I met Mrs Donnolly at the shops the other day. I wouldn't have recognised her after all these years but she came up to me, and told me how sorry she was; like so many people she wanted to tell me about you, how good it had been knowing you, what a great loss she knew you would be to me. She remembered the time you spent in the library with her, and how you helped her. We recalled the party; this remembering of moments of the past with people you hardly know is very moving.

Another day in the library I met the painter – remember he did your bedroom in that fabulous colour called Library Red – and he asked after you. When I told him he was very sad, kept saying how sorry he was, how lovely you were.

Today I went to town to do errands and into Laura Ashley to pick up some pillowslips I'd ordered, to go with a doona cover I'd bought half price. Narelle was there, who designed your wardrobe, and the linen press, and the renovations in the laundry – of course I didn't remember who she was, she had to tell me. She was as chatty and nice as usual. She left that firm, remember she wasn't the person to finish the job, she left because they kept failing to do her new kitchen. The thought flashed into my head – Lucy will be interested to hear this. I suppose because in recent years I was the one out and about and would bring home stories for you; I can't get out of the habit. Only a flash did the thought last. Narelle knew you'd died and took my hand and said lovely things. How lively you were. How we two sparked off one another.

I could write this letter forever. I do it because it might help me. I am not sure that it does. I think it might make me sadder. Anyway, it comes with all my love, always.

~

Speaking of letters, I got a lovely one from David Brooks, quite some time later. He apologised for the lateness, but I didn't mind that, it was lovely to have this later reminder. He sent a poem, not a poem about you exactly but a poem for you. More words for Lucy.

Here it is.

Puzzled Light

I.M. Lucy Halligan

Late this morning, when I heard that you had died,
I was driving into the mountains
with T, after her long flight from Europe.

We were only half-way through the ninety bends
and the traffic was bad. I'd scarcely had time to think
before my sister called
to tell me about her first grandchild
born just an hour after dawn.
The house, when we arrived, was like the *Marie Celeste*,
doors open and the car still there
but no-one in sight
until Alan emerged from somewhere below
with a sack full of garden waste – pulled weeds, pulled
heads of flowers, tree-fern fronds –
then went back down, calling for Eve,
into the thick shadow by the pond.
After they left we showered and went to bed.
Later, watching her sleep,
I could see T's eyes
darting beneath their lids
as if she were chasing something through her Slovenian dark.
I got up and wandered about the empty rooms
carefully, like an over-filled glass,
as if the light itself had just arrived.
Birdcalls I didn't recognise – it's been so long – travelled
from branch to branch, echoing across the valley,
and the wind was like distant traffic in the trees;
the tips of the tall pines
blazed bright green in the afternoon sun
and on the ground below them
magpies and brown finches
stalked strangely through the puzzled light.
I thought of you then, then of my niece, Natasha,
whom I've not seen for years,

and who has just had a daughter.
Suddenly I missed my own, terribly.
Births, and a death, it's so often like this, beginnings
and endings confused. Sometimes the richness
and the mystery of creation
are almost too much for the mind to bear.
She has woken now, and the birds are still there:
kookaburras, lowries, king parrots, currawongs.
I am always amazed at how sound
carries in the evening air, and the late colours shine.
In the gathering dusk the trunks of the pines
are something solid and abiding.
It's hard not to let the heart
calm and be held by them.
Goodbye, Lucy, goodbye.

Confidante

The thing about Lucy was that people told her things. Years ago we had a cleaning lady whose life was a catalogue of the disasters that can befall a human being. The first day she came she told Lucy that her daughter's boyfriend died the night before, asthma it was. Of course it wasn't, it was drugs. She finally admitted this. His grandma wanted to bury him in Wagga but somehow the body got lost. Her son had had troubles of a more or less criminal nature but had found Jesus and was now a fundamentalist Christian. The daughter went storming up the street to bawl out the neighbours who stole her giant marijuana plant.

She didn't tell me these stories. Lucy passed all of them on to me. I would be upstairs in the study working, she would be sitting at her desk, writing, reading, keeping herself busy as she did, and the cleaning lady would slope in with some gruesome tale that I would then hear after she had left, I never heard them direct. I always felt she was an alter ego to me, had I not had good and loving parents, been clever, educated, given opportunities. Probably because she was born in the same year as me. She got pregnant at sixteen, and ended up in a Dickensian home for unmarried mothers, doing laundry; after the baby was born she ran away with the boyfriend of one of the other girls, on his motorbike. She lost children to welfare, and the love of her life to a neglected industrial accident. She went bankrupt over a dodgy credit scheme, and got done for drink driving – I only had a few beers and a couple of Baileys, she said. Her daughter was a figure of horrified contemplation for Lucy: first the dead boyfriend, then the one in gaol; when he got out he painted their bedroom, his side black, hers pink, and went back to his burgling career. But don't worry, she said, he doesn't do it here on the northside. Only south of the lake. I'm not sure if he was the one who bashed the daughter so thoroughly she needed plastic surgery.

This was rich material, and I told her story in a piece I did for an anthology edited by Dale Spender called *Weddings and Wives*, not in any way critically but as a narrative that happened. She stopped being a cleaning lady – she was an excellent one – when her daughter got a really good job as a receptionist at 'one of those places in Fyshwick', which everybody in Canberra knows means a brothel, since they were legalised and moved to light industrial areas. She was going to mind her daughter's baby, that is have her to sleep at her house, for a good fat sum. The father was in gaol. When she told us the money the daughter was getting we doubted it was as a receptionist that she was working.

Those days were great fun. After the cleaning lady had gone Lucy and I would have lunch and with great glee she would recount the next instalment. Lucy loved stories of other people's lives, especially ones like this that she never in a fit would have lived. She would write too – diaries and stories – to capture these lives.

Lucy's voice

My agent, Margaret Connolly, reminded me what a lovely voice Lucy had. She used to talk to her on the phone quite often, since Lucy often answered the phone, either because I was away or I was working. She was my personal assistant. Margaret remembers her beautiful melodious voice, not at all the voice of a sick person, she said. Lucy loved the telephone, and talking to people, she and Margaret would have great conversations. She had a funny and confident persona on the phone.

I remember one evening, it was after six o'clock, and Nancy had called in, and we were sitting round the kitchen table having a glass of white wine. (This is the room that the architect said, Don't call it a kitchen you eat in, call it a dining room you cook in. It's a beautiful room, with a high sloping ceiling, a lovely light, and the garden through sets of French windows.) It can't have been Lent, Nancy doesn't drink wine in Lent. The phone rang and Lucy answered it, as was her wont. I could tell it wasn't anybody I knew – and what business person rings after six o'clock! Lucy said in her elegant way, No, I am afraid Marion isn't available, she's in a meeting.

Nancy and I choked with laughter. We managed to keep it in until Lucy had politely taken a message, which she wrote down in the day book, and then we shrieked with delight. Lucy looked smug, she knew she had given a great performance. After that it became a family joke; when I had a glass of wine with friends, I was in a meeting.

But Margaret remembers great conversations with Lucy, partly about business, which would have been why she rang in the first place, but also just lovely chats. Lucy's inquiring mind, her interest in the world, in words and language, her experiences of travel, made her a terrific talker, and Margaret is very fond of good talk.

Once when the phone rang we picked up simultaneously, I upstairs, Lucy downstairs. Hello, we said, at the same moment. A peremptory voice said, Please decide who's answering this phone, and the other one go away. It was Gough Whitlam, we knew without him saying so. Lucy melted away. I was chair of the Word Festival at the time and we'd asked him to be patron; he was ringing up to say yes. That became part of Lucy's repertoire of stories.

She did a marvellous job of being my personal assistant. She was terrific at answering the phone and taking messages. She did the BAS and the tax. I would have liked to pay her, but Centrelink had filled her with terror. By this time she lived on a disability pension. She'd done a tiny job for writer and historian Cassandra Pybus, as a research assistant, organised through La Trobe University. She worked about two hours a week. They were very slow to pay, it took about two months, and then they paid the whole lot in a lump. Centrelink claimed this was her weekly salary, and stopped her pension for quite a long period of time. She tried to explain to them how it worked, she had her pay slip, but they would not listen. She did not want to risk this happening again. I couldn't talk her into trying to explain to Centrelink that I was paying her a small weekly amount. This would have suited me as a tax deduction. So instead I bought her clothes from Pink Ink, shoes, various things that she wanted. She didn't expect to be paid, anyway, she liked working for me. And she lived rent free, and was fed; I hate to think how anyone could have managed out in the hard world.

For quite a long time after she died I left her mobile phone charged, and would ring her up just to hear her beautiful voice saying she was Lucy Halligan and couldn't come to the phone at the moment, please leave a message and she would ring back. Such a pleasure that was, but after a while I stopped. Knowing she never would ring back was too sad.

Tilba | 11 May 2006

Have just been to Tilba, to have a close look at it for the novel *The Apricot Colonel*. Lucy didn't know about him, of course. Felt like writing a detective novel. He lives down there in a house called the Cliffhanger. Found the kind of place his house could be, with the great rocks and the falling away of the land. Visited our friends at the Tilba Lake Community, had a walk around the property, looked at the sea and the ravines planted with Norfolk Island pines. Examined the two tiny cemeteries, one Catholic, one Protestant, on their headland facing the ocean; when they stand up at the Day of Judgment they will all be looking towards the sea, and the rising sun. Stayed in the Green Gables bed and breakfast, run impeccably by a couple of charming men.

But what I liked best was walking round the two Tilbas and remembering going there with Lucy. It was when we were staying at Isola, the philanthropist Neilma Sidney's house, which is just south of Bermagui, and several times, maybe three I think, Lucy drove us up to Tilba, which is actually Tilba Tilba, the name meaning windy, and repeating it of course meaning really windy. We had a small lunch and wandered round the shops, the nursery, the cute objects shop and the junk place. Lucy loved shopping. She couldn't choose to do a lot with nature, it demanded too much physical effort of her, though she liked to sit and contemplate it. But shopping was one of the few things she could excel at, especially on that small village scale, she could wander, and sit, examine things, admire them, buy odd stuff. Sometimes I knew we could do without things, but I never had the heart to say so. She bought an etched glass ball as big as a grapefruit; a pretty fragile thing, it sits in its perfect uselessness on a windowsill. Every now and then I wash it in soapy water and polish it with a linen cloth, and remember the pleasure she took in buying it.

This visit to Tilba brings all this back, her delight in driving there – Lucy loved driving, she did it very well, and knew it, and was proud of it; it was one of the few physical skills she had in greater measure than most people – the way she laughed with happiness as we sped up the highway, the anticipation with which she parked the car – always seeming to find a place just where she wanted to be – her good humour and fun as we wandered about. Central Tilba is a European-looking village, old wooden houses with gables, brightly painted, strung close together along a ridge, the land falling away behind them on both sides. They can easily be criticised and made fun of as commercial tourist lures, and we did plenty of that, but she bought things too. Cards at the New Age shop, with its odours of incense and soap, pickled onions for me (called Bum Hummers, too hot for Lucy) at the old cheese factory, earrings, a painted wooden angel, birthday presents for her god daughter, a scarf.

This time, walking down the street at Central Tilba, not buying anything – I have decided I have all the objects I will ever need – having really bad coffee with our friends, wandering through the nursery and succumbing to a camellia with a myriad of tiny flower buds and a hellebore which I hope is different from the ones I have (buying plants doesn't count as things), Lucy was close beside me, her laugh, her pleasure, her simple happiness in ordinary things, and I was full of delight to be in this place that she still inhabited so joyously.

~

Thinking of Lucy and shopping: she loved buying the groceries. I got a credit card for her and she would go and stock up. She was a thrifty and clever shopper. She'd go to the local supermarket and come home with all sorts of goodies which she would cook – she didn't carry them but would leave them there for the shop to deliver. A young man called Dmitri would come striding into the kitchen and heave the box of stuff down on the kitchen table. It was like a lucky dip. How spoilt I was.

Disco ball

I always used to say I wanted a disco ball. When I saw one on the television, or in a movie, I would say, Ah, a disco ball, what I really want in life is a disco ball. I saw a whole shop window full of them once, in Rundle Mall in Adelaide, I think it was. I said to people, I have seen a whole shop window full of disco balls, every kind imaginable. But I did not think of going in and buying one. I am not sure how much I really did want one and how much it was just a yearning sort of thing to say, and unexpected in the serious person I seem to be, something that I knew would never happen and so it could stand for all the things you think it would be nice to have and know you never will, really.

But Lucy listened, and for my birthday the year she died she gave me one. I was delighted at the time, and now I am even more so. Straightaway I hung it in the window of my study, which faces due north. In the summer the sun shines down directly and does not catch it, but in the other three seasons, as soon as it moves a little off its most southern meridian the sun strikes it and fills the room with little pellets of light. Over the ceiling, the walls, the bookshelves, are shining coins, ovals, dashes of radiance. They sprinkle like sequins. Where they are caught by the spines of books they have rich emerald and ruby colours like cabochon jewels.

It doesn't happen all day, and not every day. But when it does I gaze on them and think of Lucy's loving heart. How she delighted in giving people presents and searched for just the right ones. I remember the large box, about twenty-five centimetres square, and wondering what it could be. I remember my joy as I opened it: a sphere, studded with a mosaic of mirrors, fragmented but perfect. I have always wanted a disco ball, and here it is, a gift of love. Now it is April again, and my birthday; when I watch the paillettes of light quivering, or swirling crazily round the room when I nudge my ball, I think of Lucy. A shower of light, and she is there in it. Her presence fills the room.

PS – The brilliant designer Sandy Cull had the idea of using this image on the cover of this book. So poignant.

Painted toenails | 2000

The plane got in early in the morning and we went straight to the hotel. The room was dark, and musty with new cleaning. We pulled the curtains and there, hanging in the sky, hazy, gauzy pink in the thick dawn atmosphere was the Parthenon. We were in Athens and yet it was entirely surprising that it should be there, we'd had such a sense of the tumbling city all about us. Lucy was thrilled, so was I. She had been overseas a number of times before, to France and England and briefly to Italy, but that was as part of the family. Now the two of us were travelling in new fields.

A sure way to enrage her was to tell her about things she had seen which she had no memory of. Her study of fine art at university involved the Byzantine period and the mosaics of Ravenna; she fell in love with them. She'd been there when she was five but had absolutely no memory of that. The reason, we understood, was her two bouts of open-heart surgery, both involving the heart-lung machine; as I've said, this plays havoc with the memory. Somehow taking your blood out of your body and passing it through a machine changes things in your brain, and gives you those very strange dreams I have mentioned. Even without this, recalling things from her early childhood could have been difficult, but as it was, not a hope. It quite broke her heart that she had seen these marvellous creations and had no memory of them. I'd hoped that she would go back to Ravenna one day but it didn't happen.

But we made it to Greece and Turkey. Our friend Jill organised the tour, of a group of people many of whom knew one another, a lot of them my ex-colleagues from teaching days. Lucy was the youngest, by far, the rest were mostly my age or older. Everything was organised: accommodation, bus tours, a lot of meals, visits to museums, galleries, architectural sites. Normally I don't like to travel like this, I like to make my own way, in my own time, not tightly timetabled, staying more or less lengthily in places, and usually choosing to spend more time doing a few things than trying to cram everything in.

But that was in countries where I knew the language, and the culture. I did not think that Lucy and I would be able to make our own way in these Greek and Turkish places, so the conducted tour was a great idea. We even succeeded in getting out of bed and having our bags packed every day.

Later that day in Athens we walked up the Parthenon and Lucy got to the top. I had not expected she would, had supposed she would sit on a stone and wait for the party to come back. But she climbed all the way which was very thrilling for her, and made me so happy. And quite often she achieved what seemed for her superhuman feats; her lungs made walking for long difficult, since she did not get enough oxygen for sustained effort. One of the women on the tour said she thought she imagined how Lucy felt; once she had been high in the Andes and suffered from oxygen deprivation, and understood how unpleasant it was.

We went to all the expected places: Delphi, Olympus, Samos. One morning, we were at Samos, sat under the trees looking at ruins. It was expected that we would have coffee, but the kiosk had half bottles of Samian wine and we couldn't resist the poetic weight of this – isn't it Keats who has Samian wine? Actually, it turns out to be Byron who filled high the cup of Samian wine. Some of the tour joined us, others looked askance. The wine was light and mild and a great historical-literary experience. That's what we told ourselves.

We went on a big car ferry and a small boat. We saw Ephesus, starting at the top of the hill and walking down. Lucy managed wonderfully well. We ate some fine meals, became connoisseurs of Greek salads, and got very fond of ouzo.

Everybody got fond of Lucy. Her courage was one thing, but mainly her humour endeared her. She was always good tempered and full of jokes. Her youth helped, and the fact that the older people were so much healthier, they worried about her. In Turkey we travelled on a *gulet*, a handsome rather classical sort of boat which we slept on; we needed two for our party of about eighteen. We had our meals on deck, simple food, a lot of meat stews with yoghurt, and quite often barley, which was delicious in this context, and usually a little sliced fruit for dessert. You could buy wine of a modest kind. Some travellers were critical of this food; it was wholesome and nourishing and not fancy; they wanted more variety. Really they meant they wanted more expensive food, but it had been negotiated to a certain price, and that was it. Some days as we sailed around we would anchor in a bay and go to a restaurant; one was in a place that seemed deserted and served wonderful fish. We always anchored overnight, and during the day sailed close to the shore, past lonely landscapes of whitish grey rock and scrubby vegetation, and imagined Ulysses seeing it just like this. Sometimes we swam from the boat; not Lucy, who wasn't a swimmer. I went in, the water was cold, and perfectly clear, you could see down, far far down, maybe that dim shape below was a wrecked ship from the Trojan war.

The cabin was stuffy and stank of diesel oil so we took our bedclothes and slept on deck; there was a big padded cushion on a wide seat which was as big as a double bed. It was in the bow of the boat and the crew climbed over us when we set sail very early next morning but we put our heads under the bedclothes and nobody seemed to mind. We'd open our eyes and admire the dawn and go back to sleep until people started getting up. It was wonderful sleeping out, the air fresh, cool, not at all cold; it was April and still spring.

One day we were moored in a deserted shapely bay, the boats some fifty metres apart, I suppose. Some people from one swam over and visited us. Lucy was painting her toenails on deck. Fascinating; most of the women had had nothing to do with painted toenails before. Suddenly Lucy was painting everyone's toenails. They loved it, it made them feel very sexy. When you first paint your toenails that is how you feel, as though it is a kind of primping of the body for erotic purposes. The visitors had to wait until their nails dried before they swam back to their boat.

One of Lucy's good friends, from the boarding house at my school (I say good friend though she had only met her on the trip; there were a lot of people who learnt to love her very quickly), had taken the kayak and was paddling round the bay; she kept popping into view as she circled far away, in and around the promontories and small islands, a tiny shape in the distance. She was very sporting, loved to play golf and tennis. She died not long after that trip, of a very fast-moving cancer; she was the next youngest after Lucy. At her memorial service we remembered her, the small shape valiantly paddling across the pale green waters of the bay.

Another woman on the trip was working at the school when I first started teaching. She was very fierce, the kids were very respectful of her; I was quite scared of her myself. She and Lucy developed an elaborate game where whenever they saw one another each day they had a kind of competition for who could come up with the most fulsome endearments. Oh darling sweetheart honeybun cutie-pie, more and more extravagant every day. They laughed their heads off at this. I always felt a kind of amazement about it.

Then Lucy wasn't very well. We had antibiotics but put off taking them, she was so healthy it seemed she might throw off this small cold. But suddenly she was much worse. This all happened in about half a day. Some people thought it might be sleeping outside; I didn't, we were perfectly warm and the air was so much healthier than down in the smelly cabin. We pulled into Marmara and Lucy lay asleep on the big cushion in the front of the boat. The crew made her a yoghurt drink they said would make her better; it was very good, but didn't. So we called the doctor. I remember waiting for him, standing on the ladder at the front of the boat, looking high up the hill at the bar where everybody had gone to have a drink, and stood waving down at us. Me and one other person who didn't feel well either. I went across to a cafe on the wharf and they sent over two meals of grilled lamb. Lucy wasn't eating. Then the doctor came. Pleurisy, he said, and sent an ambulance to take her to hospital.

It was a small private hospital named after a young woman who had died for lack of good medical care; her family had set it up in her memory, to save others. We saw a doctor who was short, portly, full of importance, with not a lot of English.

This was always a nightmare occasion, seeing a doctor who did not know anything about Lucy. We had letters from her heart specialist, but they didn't really help. The problem was that listening to her heart, discovering how it worked, always gave them such a fright. They could not believe it. I would tell them yes, it's not good, but it functions for her, she lives with it, she can cope. She has tremendous stamina. She just needs treatment to get rid of this pleurisy, forget the heart. But of course they couldn't. He asked could he make some x-rays for his own use, he wanted to study this interesting case. Lucy said yes; we thought we should be helpful. It was a bargain we were making with him.

But he was not a generous man, and could not really cope. He got her on to intravenous antibiotics, and ventolin inhalers. Whereas in Australia the ventolin spray comes through a plastic mask that you strap to your face, which directs it very precisely and is thrown away each time, here it came out of a tube and a lot of it dissipated into the air. We knew it was lack of funds that caused this. You didn't get hot water until late in the day, they did not turn it on till then. The room was hot, and Lucy has always suffered from the heat; we put the air conditioner on. The first thing the doctor did when he came was turn it off. We turned it back on when he went. He claimed it was not good for her but I knew it was economy.

During this time I was staying in a nearby hotel, a new rather jerry-built but very cheap and quite comfortable place. I realised Marmara was a great spot for English package tours; there were a lot of lobster-pink overweight Brits lounging around. The hotel had the delicious Turkish breakfasts we had become used to, ham and cold meats, cheeses, marvellous great bowls of thick plain yoghurt, small vats of honey, jams, fruit, breads, cakes, juices, the cherry especially good, coffee. There were a whole lot of English people eating breakfast, but not this, which was included in the tariff; they were having bacon and eggs, which you had to pay for. How mad, I thought.

Some people from the tour came in taxis on the first morning to visit, bringing little presents for Lucy. They seemed shocked.

The first evening I looked out the hotel window and saw a great screen being erected in the beer garden below. Not immediately did I realise that it was to watch the World Cup, which was happening in Sweden or somewhere. Very late. Turkey won. There was much loud celebration and people drove round all night singing, shouting, honking car horns. Very little sleep for anyone that night.

I had vouchers to have dinner in the doctors' canteen. Cafeteria style: you picked up a large oblong stainless steel tray with square and round hollows in it and food was dolloped into it. More of the delicious spicy stews, sometimes meat, mainly vegetables. Lots of eggplant and courgettes, cucumber salads. Yoghurt. Greek salad. Simple food, very healthy. No chips or junk. I would keep a bottle of wine at the hotel and have a glass when I went back, after Lucy had settled for the night.

It was a funny life. Sort of terrifying. Busy. A huge dark panic hanging over you but daily life very full of things to do, visiting Lucy, keeping her cheered. Making phone calls. We watched the television and saw on the BBC news the Sorry march across the Sydney Harbour Bridge. Otherwise Australia didn't get mentioned.

The rest of the tour finished its *gulet* trip and then went off on the ferry to Rhodes. Lucy was getting better, I could see that she was, I knew she would when she was treated. She felt better. I said to the doctor I thought she would be well enough to go on soon. No, he said, she must go to Istanbul and fly back to Australia.

The rest of the tour was back on the mainland and was making its way by bus up to Cappadocia. The guide, a very charming young man who liked Lucy and often stayed and chatted with her when she sat and rested instead of rushing about with the others, kept in touch with us and had organised for another guide, a young woman, to look after us in Marmara. She made the travel arrangements. She was a very sweet person, and gave Lucy a pretty key ring with a fascinating stone in it.

The doctor was clear that he wasn't very happy with Lucy's going, but he agreed that it was okay. The young guide came with us to the airport, a three-hour drive. When we got there the airport authorities would not let us fly. The doctor had rung up and said they were to refuse her permission, on the grounds that something might go wrong. What, we asked? It was a shortish flight, straight to Ankara, we would be there quickly, she was perfectly all right. We talked and talked, through the guide, but it did no good. Back three hours to Marmara. We went and saw the doctor. He smiled greasily and waved his hands about. He was adamant in a sickly smiling way. I did not think he had Lucy's wellbeing truly at heart. I suspected he wanted her back for the income she was bringing him. And indeed I did pay him a great deal of money, which the insurance mostly covered.

He said *Off yourssie*, several times. Whatever did he mean? His assistant explained, with a certain embarrassment, that this was a joke, pronouncing 'of course' as though they were Turkish words.

The lovely young guide took us to another heart doctor in the public hospital. She examined Lucy carefully and readily gave her agreement. So to the airport again; another three hours. Nine hours car drive to and from. Instead of three. I was so angry with the doctor for putting her through this frightful travelling, in the name of looking after her.

We flew to Istanbul, waited, changed planes, flew to Ankara, arriving about midnight, then driving for more than two hours to get to Cappadocia. Without that doctor we'd have been there in the early afternoon, on a direct flight. Jill had given the desk staff orders to call her when we arrived, she came down and welcomed us back.

We slept in next day and then they brought Lucy to where the group was having lunch. She got a kind of standing ovation. I saw a bit of Cappadocia and its strange cave dwellings; Lucy looked from the bus.

And so we went on, finishing the tour as we had planned. Lucy took things easy, but had a great time. She liked people more than she did places, and she was welcomed back to the group with such delight. Our guide paid special attention. I remember the two of them sitting on a bench in the Topkapi Palace chattering away. She had no relapse, and was in terrific health for the rest of the journey. That Turkish doctor had no idea of her stamina or her willpower or her tenacity; we'd told him but he just listened to her heart and did not believe us.

We went from Istanbul to Paris, where we met James, and then spent a week in Paris and some weeks with a hire car travelling and in Sévérac. Lucy even drove, but not much. It was James who zipped us through the countryside, on busy single carriageway roads with great trucks that you had to pass without losing momentum; essentially a job for a young person I thought, as I averted my eyes.

I had sold our lovely old Citroën CX that we had bought in 1976; it was twenty-five years old. It was very beautiful and I got enough money to pay their fares and hire the car. We went back to old haunts. Sévérac was Lucy's nearly favourite place in all the world, we all have always loved it. They were two and five when they first went there, later they went to school there, and they were all very happy times. We spent days in Voulx with our dear friend Grant, remembering the past and loved ones who had died: Grant's partner, Bernard, and Graham, his friend, my husband, their father. We sat at the dinner table and ate great meals and talked about them, and wept sometimes. It got late and I went to bed, but the three of them stayed up, opening another bottle of wine, celebrating their friendship.

PS – At Lucy's funeral several women from the tour came up to me and said, secretly, I painted my toenails, in memory of Lucy.

LEGACY

The shell

Several years later Lucy was in hospital in Canberra with a severe chest infection that made her very sick. She had to sleep sitting up which was horribly uncomfortable but less so than lying down. That's when we got her on to oxygen. I've told the story of the counsellor called Margaret whom we had all talked to when we were sad or full of loss; she went to see Lucy. It was impossible to find comforting things to say, like you will be better soon, hang on it will all be over shortly; it was not at all certain that it would be. That's when Margaret gave her the long curled shell to hold, saying, When you feel miserable, hold this, and it will comfort you, you will know we are thinking of you.

It was a brilliant idea, it worked, it comforted her. In fact she got better, and the trip we'd planned – my going by plane to the Byron Bay Writers Festival, her flying up to join me when it had finished, and us hiring a car, driving to friends at Springbrook and then on to Brisbane to stay with Rosie – happened after all, though all the doctors had looked scandalised and pitying when we'd hoped that it might. She did all the driving. She had remarkable resilience, remarkable stamina. She needed them, to survive with her maladies.

After she died the doctor said it could have happened at any time, that her heart could have just stopped, like that. I'm glad it didn't when we were doing 110 down a motorway.

But after this I began to realise that when she got one of her chest infections she did not get as well as she had been before it, that there was a gradual decline. I saw it as a matter of steps, she would go down three or four steps and manage to climb back only two, so she kept getting just a little worse. She needed more and more cortisone to get her lungs functioning.

This was when the doctors started talking about the heart-lungs-liver transplant that so filled her with horror. And also mentioning that this might not be possible, she might not be well enough to support it. It was a strange gloomy time, with us both thinking things we didn't ever say.

And I realise, not thinking things that maybe I ought to have thought, about where this was all going to go. We lived in the present, trying to enjoy things as they happened, not asking fruitless questions like, Where is all this going to end? She had always pulled through in the past, however bad the situation; we held on to that.

Lament

We often have cause to lament the fact that Lucy did not live long enough to meet Bianca. She would be so excited by her, so enjoy her company, find her so funny. For example, we went to a big exhibition about Renaissance painting at the National Gallery of Australia. When John and I used to have Bianca all day Monday, when she was at day care four days a week, we'd often go to the gallery. There were a lot of madonnas and children in this exhibition, and Bianca at the time was keen on mothers and babies. She walked around and looked.

Is the baby Jesus a boy or a girl? she asked.

What do you think? I asked, pointing to one of the paintings.

She went and looked. A boy, she said. He's got a penis.

Afterwards at lunch, when she was hoeing into a smoked salmon sandwich, she said, in that high clear penetrating voice that small children can have: Baby Jesus's got a penis. Daddy's got a penis. I haven't got a penis. I've got a bagina. Have you got a bagina, Granny?

Yes, I muttered.

There were three businessmen at the next table. Have they got a penis? said Bianca.

At this point I decided it was time to change the subject.

This sort of thing is not exactly fun at the time, but it's amusing in recollection.

Now she's eight, and very firm and strong-minded and serious and full of purpose. She would not dream of talking about private parts in public, though she knows the vocabulary. No stupid pseudo euphemisms like 'front bottom' for her. And she's certainly sorted out her 'b's and 'v's. She doesn't like to eat cake or sugary foods (not very often) and she can fulminate magnificently about food from McDonald's. *Disgusting*, she says, absolutely *disgusting*. Plastic, industrial, *junk*. She will never eat it. I agree with her but it was not me who taught her this.

One of her favourite activities is reading. When she comes to me after school a good thing to do is silent reading. We lie on Lucy's rattly brass bed and silent read. When I told her that I had read an article by a schoolteacher complaining that lots of teenagers couldn't silent read she was aghast. Perhaps they can't read at all, she said. When we have silent reading at school a lot of the boys don't do it, they chitter-chatter. (This is certainly a quote, I suppose, from her teacher.)

Oh, say I, what do they talk about?

Video games, she says, with immense scorn.

When she has a sleepover at my place she likes to spend the night in Lucy's bed. It used to be that she wanted to sleep with me, and John would go down to Lucy's bed, but these days she's very keen. I love to see her beautiful blonde head lying on the pillow, with the doona tucked round her chin.

Now, she's having a baby brother. She is very excited about this, and I think she will look after him wonderfully. He will take his place on the family tree, which is wonderfully rogue.

How Lucy would have enjoyed this.

The new baby is a boy. I think this is a good thing. If he were a girl Bianca could be an impossibly hard act to follow.

Josie | 2 March 2008

Back from Perth, from the literary festival. John picked up Josie from the cattery. Ten days she was there, a long time. Too long a time to be left at home on her own. The Curlies next door feed her, assiduously, and talk to her, stroke her, but still she is an old lady now, fifteen years old; what if something went wrong? We know she is safe there.

John brings her inside in her travelling box. She is out in a quick sinuous slide and walks round the house, round and round, checking that everything is there. We open the back door and she goes in and out, walking round the garden, sits on the mat inside and the mat outside, gazing. The cattery is quite a classy one, she had a room with a veranda, but it is nothing like a whole house and garden.

We take the weekend papers and sit outside since we know she likes company. She has a habit of sitting nearby with her back to us, totally aware of our presence. Or else she sits on a chair, or even better, on the paper you are reading. After a while James comes round. Don't move, he says, and sits down to read the papers too. There is still some coffee so he has that. Once I would have opened a bottle of wine, it's late enough, but not now that he is keeping Julee company on her no alcohol in pregnancy regime. No chore for Julee, who's not much interested in wine, harder work for him. Josie is pleased to see him, and he gives her a long pat; she was once his cat. The last of her tribe, he calls her. All those years ago, when he was living in a group house in Ainslie, a good friend's cat had kittens and each tenant of the house took one. None of them lived very long. Josie is the only one still alive, so grand and full of years.

I say that the girl in the cattery remarked how very glossy and well-kept Josie is, especially for a cat her age. She was always pretty, with her tortoiseshell tabby markings and her pointed wide-eyed face, and her coat is still thick and silky, her bib and paws dazzling white.

Ah, says James, that's because she was so well-loved. Remember how Lucy doted on her. She was the most loved cat in the world.

They passed a good part of their days in bed together. Lucy didn't always spend all her days in bed, but she always had a rest, or a nap, or watched television, and Josie curled up close with her. Or else at the kitchen table; Lucy found her a bit heavy on her lap, so Josie would curl up on the table in front of her and Lucy would cuddle her, as though she were nursing her. She adored her. Used to talk loving nonsense to her. We would tease her about little old ladies and their cats. She got treated pretty robustly, Lucy did.

She is Lucy's legacy, I said. We have been faithful.

I am aware of this, often. I think of it in these grand words, that it is something left to us, that has to be done. I never would let Josie sleep on my bed, that glossy coat comes off in great quantities of fur, plus a good lot of garden grot. Pigpen, I call her, after the character in *Peanuts* who goes everywhere in a cloud of dust. I would shoo her off. Go back to Lucy, I would say. But now I let her sleep on the bed. John is very good about it; he has got attached to her too. He is mostly the one who feeds her, being soft-hearted and giving in to her demands. There was little enough room when I slept alone, now it is a crowd. It is like having a large and furry cannonball taking up much of the bed's surfaces. She would sleep with her head on the pillow if we let her. I am not sure whether she thinks she is a person or that we are big cats. Sometimes in the night she feels affectionate and purrs like a powerful dynamo. She gets up before dawn to go to the loo, like the rest of us, comes back and jumps straight on to our sleeping bodies, landing with all her weight on her four pointed paws. Often she decides to have a major wash and the whole bed vibrates with the energy of it. I used to remark that you would go into Lucy's room and there would be the cat luxuriating in the whole bed while Lucy hung from her fingernails to the outside edge. I'm making Josie sound like an enormous beast but actually she is quite small and delicate, plumpish but not very. She is a most beautiful, tranquil and loving cat. I think she is so affectionate because Lucy made her like that. We will be heartbroken when she dies.

The day after she came home we found a mouse in the back garden, lying on the paved area. Quite a big mouse, very dead, no visible wounds. We thanked her for it, grateful that she hadn't brought it inside as a real present – the last one she left on the mat beside the computer table. She carried it all the way upstairs as a true gift of affection.

Over the years we have had a number of these. Under the kitchen table, in the hallway. Once on the Afghan carpet in the sitting room. It was very well camouflaged. Very battered. Lucy stood on it. She had bare feet. She yelled and yelled and yelled. Graham was trying to sell our old Holden station wagon which she wasn't very happy about, she loved driving it. The young man considering buying it showed a certain dismay at all the wailing. I had to rush her into the bathroom, hopping on one leg, and scrub and scrub and scrub the offended foot. You could always make her shudder, remembering the mouse on the carpet. More recently one was left on our bedroom floor, right where John steps when he gets out of bed in the dark. Miraculously, he missed it.

Two days after the post-Perth kill, another mouse, this one with its middle all eaten away. I nearly stood on it; was walking across the paving stones and suddenly saw where my foot was about to land. I yanked it back and up and then forward another twenty centimetres or so, a manoeuvre I was impressed by my ability to perform and which jarred my hip quite unpleasantly.

The mice are small and quite pretty fieldmice that come down from the mountain looking for food. So we tell ourselves. There's a lot of undergrowth for them to live in. Clearly Josie was celebrating being back home with a little hunting.

I daresay it was a case that while the cat was away, the mice had been playing.

The dog | 2016

Bianca now has a dog. Probably, more accurately, daddy now has a dog. Both are thrilled. He's a Staffordshire terrier, because when James was in Newcastle in the nineties being a rock musician, very successfully though not at quite the same level as Silverchair, who had the advantage of being little more than children, so their mothers had to travel to gigs with them, at that time he had a Staffy called Holly, whom he loved dearly. When he parted from his girlfriend she kept the dog, which quite broke James's heart, and now there is Charlie. He is being brought up strictly, not allowed up the stairs, no sleeping on beds, and so on. Though at the moment they are at the coast, and Charlie is I believe sleeping in Bianca's room, but in his own bed. They romp about and roll around and go for long walks. Bianca says she would like a cat too; maybe when their very old and frail cat Chai dies, she can get a kitten.

Cats | 2005

Josie is bereft. She demands affection all the time, not just from me, from complete strangers she would normally not even speak to. She was so much Lucy's cat, had such constant and ungrudging love from her, she cannot quite believe it is no longer there.

For months afterwards she would not even go into Lucy's room. She walked past, occasionally glancing out of the corner of her eye, but she never took even a step towards it. She stayed with Lucy after she died; when James came and found his sister, lying on the bed with a peaceful sleeping expression on her face, Josie was curled up beside her. We felt pleased that Lucy had this company. Even when there were police and fire and ambulance people and doctors milling about, Josie stayed. (These are all the people who turn up when someone dies unexpectedly.) And then never put paw over the threshold. Until I took her to the vet to have her annual shots, and she came home and curled up in Lucy's room in a tiny space between a chest and the bookcase, a place she never had been in before. We discovered that the warm air from the heating vent channels under the chest and it is a hot spot. She still goes there sometimes. And curls up on other heating outlets. One is in the sun as well. On these occasions she is almost too hot to touch, her fur burns with heat.

Otherwise she is on our bed, sleeping in the sunshine, and if we are in it, pushed up against us. If I am not careful I find myself teetering on the outside edge of the queen-sized bed. At night she arrives usually at five past eleven; the heating goes off at eleven, and up she comes and lands on us like that cannonball with sharp pointed feet. I have to give her as much love and attention as I can, but Lucy set a very high bar. Even the vet remarked on what a beloved cat she clearly is. That was when she sat up against the vet's chest with her arms around her neck, like a baby.

At first Lucy didn't want her. She was James's cat and when he was going to Newcastle he told Lucy she could have his cat. Her real name is Jocasta, mother of Oedipus. Like a lot of bad puns in cat names it has got lost. Now she is Josie, or Joey, or Josephina, or Jellybones, sometimes Bones for short. Lucy also called her Chelsea and various other names I have forgotten. Anyway Lucy said she did not want his cat. She was still sad about Camille, who turned out to be a monster and had to be put down, but Lucy grieved for him.

Camille was in a tradition of our cats, named for heroines out of the *Aeneas*, a long medieval poem which was the subject of Graham's PhD. The first was Lunete, little moon, a lovely Burmese. Then there was Dido, an equally beautiful Burmese, who was run over very young, and how it happened I do not know, in our quiet street and she so quick and savvy. Then there was Camilla, an Etruscan princess, who wore tiger skin and ran like the wind, which suited this cat, who was half Cornish Rex and half Siamese with barely visible stripes, and could indeed run like the wind. Only thing is, we found out after quite a bit she was a boy (we are not good at cat sexing; our first cat Tushypeg spent more than a year being a girl), which made calling him Camilla difficult. One vet had him down as Camel. When you are giving a cat a name you should always practise saying it to the vet and spelling it out for her to write down, then you will understand what is foolish. This one just had to be Camille which was always a bit embarrassing, unlike Camilla.

But Camille went mad. At first he only attacked me, racing out from behind bushes when I was in the garden and biting and scratching my legs. I was frightened of him, but the rest of the family did not take it too seriously. Much to my fury. But one night when Lucy was sitting on the sofa he crept along the back and sank his teeth and claws into her head, and then very shortly after that she woke up in bed one night and sat up in a panic, and just as she did so Camille had leapt and sprung upon the place on the pillow where her head had been. His eyes went red and mad when he did this. That was very frightening. What if that strange instinct of danger had not made her sit up so suddenly? We took him to the vet who thought he might have a brain tumour. He said we could take him to Sydney and have a CAT scan. (Everybody laughed.) But this would cost thousands of dollars. I was disenchanted with this animal, especially as he had a habit of breaking precious pots, which none of our cats before or since have ever done, they leap among them with agility and grace. And Lucy was terrified. So we had him put down. But she was still very unhappy about his loss, and did not want another cat. James brought Josie round; Lucy said, No, James, and immediately fell in love with her. She is a gentle and sweet-natured plump little tabby, a perfect little gutter cat, cuddly and contented provided she gets lots of love and attention.

And now I have not the heart to move her off my bed. She sleeps up close, preferably tucked into my tummy, or else the curve of my knees. The doona no longer functions as a puffy soft cover but is anchored as though by a stone. She leaves cat fur all over the place, though Julee does brush her when she visits, and she has a habit of dribbling. When she is happy she dribbles cupfuls. But she is so pretty, such a perfect little classical cat shape as she sits with her back elegantly turned, she charms everybody; they wipe up the dribble. Well, nearly everybody. Rosie's twins adore her. Amanda took some photographs of the flowers from Lucy's coffin laid out in the garden, and Josie sitting up close beside them. It is impossible not to think she knew what they were.

~

There is a postscript to this. When she was seventeen I took Josie to the vet because she wasn't well. The vet was worried about her teeth, and took some out. She was still worried and did tests and discovered that she had cancer in her jaw. She said she could have chemotherapy, not a very strong dose, since cats didn't understand the principle of making them ill to make them better. It was quite likely not to work. No, we said, not with an old cat like this, it would be too miserable.

We decided to take her home and see how she went. For a while she was okay. If we had to go away the vet would board her in the cat hospital for us, which made us feel she was safe. But one day I picked her up off the bed and she didn't even purr. I knew she was very ill. The vet said she would have a very bad headache. So we had her put to sleep. She sat very gently on the table while I cuddled her, did not even flinch when the vet injected her, then quickly slid into sleep and died. We sent her off to be cremated, and her ashes came back in a pottery jar with a paper flower tied to the top. So now we have Josie's ashes and Lucy's and Graham's. James says we have to do something about this. Scatter them somewhere. I don't know, I quite like having them about. One day, I suppose.

In the past we've buried our cats in the back garden. But it was dead winter, cold, the garden hard and frosty with no clear space. It was better to cremate her.

One day soon I will get another cat. Josie was such a lovely affectionate creature; when we have mourned her we will get a kitten. I think Bianca would like granny to have a kitten.

And were angel Lucy to be watching from heaven I could look her in the eye and say, I looked after your cat and loved her; she was your legacy and I did not fail. As it is, it is my satisfaction that knows this.

~

And now we have Henry, who may be a tabby-pointed Siamese. He has tabby markings, including an M over his forehead, and the slinky walk and strong body of a Siamese, with astonishing blue eyes. He's a rescue cat, was a stray, so his age and provenance have to be guessed. He wasn't actually a kitten, kittens cost a great deal of money, and when it came to the point training one seemed a lot of effort. Bianca loves him, and he her. She picks him up and hauls him around. He lets her do it, with an expression of marvellous long-suffering, though he doesn't much like being carried around, and nobody else is allowed. He likes to lean into you, on his own terms, and has the loudest purr. He's very keen on company. One day we had the plumber, the two cleaning ladies and the gardener all in one day. Henry thought this was the greatest fun, he visited them all, and rubbed up against them.

Edgar loves him too, but the cat will have nothing to do with him and is never anywhere to be found when Eddie comes over.

The first time we went away for the weekend he watched us packing with dismay. When we started putting things in the car he cried as though his heart was broken. He watched us leave through the window, looking completely desolate. We told him he wouldn't be alone for long but this didn't help. It was Friday morning, James would come after work and spend the weekend. Once James turned up Henry was perfectly happy, and now he doesn't mind when we go away, because he has learnt we will come back. He seems to know we are not abandoning him. We imagine his family must have deserted him once, and that was why he was frightened of it happening again. But before that they must have loved him; he is good at being loved, Henry is.

Lighting candles | 2005

Brenda and Rosie as they walk across the top of Spain to Compostela are lighting candles to Lucy. In the great old churches with their banks of holders, they are lighting candles for her.

They remarked that perhaps Lucy would not have thought much of this but I said, Yes, she'd have loved it. When we travelled in Greece and then in France she always lit candles to Graham. She loved rituals and understood them. No matter that she did not believe that it would help Graham in any way, she lit the candles for his sake and hers, because that was a way of thinking of him.

Now I have lighted candles in churches all over Europe. In Saint Germain des Prés, in Paris, in Sant'Appollinare in Classe in Ravenna, in a small Romanesque church on the edge of a cliff in Portovenere, which is on the Golfo dei Poeti, the poets in question being Byron and Shelley and Dante too. And this gulf is where Shelley drowned, so you are already thinking of death, sadly too young, and even younger the children that Shelley and Mary buried as they travelled, leaving behind them a trail of tiny graves. I buy Richard Holmes's *Footsteps* as an ebook, the paper one being still at home, so I can read what he said about them, and John can too. And their little Willmouse, who was four when he died in Rome, they must have thought he was safe. It's not really surprising that the babies should die, being carted around in carriages with servants and who knows what sort of hygiene, but Willmouse, that breaks your heart. A child of four is such a person; they knew that, you can tell from the way they write about him. The pain in their hearts for so many small deaths is hard to think of.

The candles flicker in draughty churches. We don't say prayers, exactly, we remember, and remembering is prayer. We pay attention, stay still, wait. I should think everybody who lights a candle does the same, they are surrounded by a powerful net of thoughts.

And again, in 2014, at Saint Sulpice in Paris and at Ely Cathedral we light candles, and pay attention. And in Hanoi, not in a church, in a courtyard, a big bundle of incense sticks, stuck into a wide pot of sand. I try to light the wrong end, the woman selling them shakes her head. I am embarrassed, it is not my ritual.

Janus-faced

If sadness for the death of a loved one were a god they would be two-faced, like Janus. Sadness is one body but there are two aspects to it. There is the grief we feel for a person, our sorrow, that squeezes the heart and shortens the breath, that fills eyes with tears and bends the shoulders under its weight. It is entirely selfish, it is my loss of the dead person that is preoccupying me, my own misery that has affected my body in this way that feels like decrepit old age suddenly come.

So, one face of the god looks in, inside the bereaved person. The other looks out, at the beloved, and mourns for the life they are missing. One day in December of 1998, shortly after Graham died, I turned the car into Majura Avenue. One of Strauss's *Four Last Songs* was playing on the radio, quite loud, and as I drove down this south-west leading road I was heading into a most brilliant sunset, with great scarves of red and gold streaming across the sky. And I felt immense sorrow that he was not here to see and hear this, to enjoy the smooth riding of the car with the music and the sunset that filled me with exhilaration for the beauty of the world. That he never would see such a thing again.

And often I think of Lucy, how she would have loved this. How she would have delighted in the wedding of James and Julee, in February 2006. And in the birth of baby Milly, her cousin Ben's daughter, in Ireland, a fine healthy baby of eleven pounds three ounces, and her mother a tiny Irish lass with creamy skin and green eyes. How she would have loved visiting James and Julee in their new house, in Downer. She went sometimes to their apartment in Turner, but it was up three flights of stairs and that was seriously difficult. She could only go when she was feeling strong enough to make the effort.

Often when I am watching the television, I think, how Lucy would have enjoyed that. *New Tricks*, for instance, the British program about old detectives brought out of retirement to solve old cases. She was a great fan of Dennis Waterman, she would have liked seeing him in that, and him singing its theme song. Or *The Last Detective*, with the actor who was one of the Doctors in *Doctor Who*, she was a fan of that program too, and of him. He was Tristan, that feckless brother in *All Creatures Great and Small*, a long time ago now. Lucy enjoyed television, and made even bad programs good fun; its narratives made up for their absence in her own life.

On the third anniversary of her death, in November 2007, the four of us, James and Julee, John and me, sat in the garden, under her rose arbour, which is a *gloriette* in French. The flowers were blooming, we had candles, and wine, and drank to her memory. Josie the cat sat with us, her back turned, guarding us. Over dinner we played Lucy's favourite ABBA songs. I know it is not fashionable to like ABBA, in my circles anyway, but it is such energetic music. When we were in Paris in the Christmas of 1976 Graham had bought her a tape of their songs, their new album, *Arrival*, and I remember sitting in the old house in the Paris suburbs, at the cold turning of the year, far from home but making our own home in this little loving knot of the four of us, with this singing, so warm and vital, making the room cosy and exciting at once. We didn't have much music, ABBA got played often. Lucy never stopped liking them; what we listened to that night was on CDs she'd bought, the tape wore out long ago. It was ABBA songs we played as people came into the crematorium, until it was time for her coffin to go, then it was Thomas Tallis's *Spem in alium*. She liked that too. Sometimes I play her CD of David Hobson singing opera, which she adored. And I listen to the old song as we sang it:

> Say did you hear my lady
> Go down the garden singing
> Silencing the blackbirds
> None so fair as she.

We used to play that on the CD player in the kitchen; I don't know why we found it so beautiful. Now tears come to my eyes when I hear its poignant notes.

Julee and James brought some cones of rose-scented incense, and an opalescent rose-coloured glass to burn them in. James thinks you should burn incense when you think about the dead. We sat in the gloriette and the scent wreathed around us.

~

Now there is the beautiful granddaughter, her niece, who will be two in a couple of weeks. She knows about Lucy. James and I both have the same photo on the wall and Bianca knows who it is, she looks at her, talks about her. When you ask her where Lucy is she bangs her chest, meaning in her heart. We can't tell her Lucy is in heaven, that would not be right, but for Bianca death means people are in our hearts. Lucy is such a beautiful word in Bianca's mouth; I wish Lucy could hear her say it. And of course it is her name too, she is Bianca Lucy.

I reiterate my envy of the Victorians: they could believe that Lucy does hear her say it, that she is in heaven and watching all of this. Sometimes I think, what if they were right? But then I think, well, they believed it because it comforted them. The loss of children was too dreadful otherwise, you had to think they were angels in heaven or it was all too miserable. We have made things much harder for ourselves.

Postscript | 22 May 2014

Looking at Bibi, how blonde she is, this must somehow come from Graham, who had blue blue eyes and reddish hair. (Bibi is Bianca's pet name, her version of her name when she first learnt to speak. The other day she said, Granny, you can call me Bibi when we are at home but when we are out with people you have to call me Bianca.

So I try to remember.) She has got Graham's wit, his passion for reading and writing and words, how he would have loved that in her. How he would have loved that her physicality is all her own. She has a sturdy, slender, strong, graceful little body, and she asks a lot of it, she constantly bends it to her will. She can't pass an iron railing without using it for monkey bars, she loves slippery dips, and going up staircases and sliding down poles. At my house she likes to use the upstairs loo, just so she can climb up and down to it. When she is on a swing she makes you afraid she is going to flip over the top. She dotes on swimming, is quick and lithe as an otter in the water. Throw her in the deep end and she'll swim around for a while then climb out. She never walks when she can run. She dances a weird hopscotch on the terracotta tiles of the kitchen floor. She loves to sit on your lap, despite her long legs; her knobbly little bottom bones stick into you. She bends seriously over her page, the perfect *bonne petite fille sage*, the good little girl, butter would turn into an ice sculpture in her mouth, and then she's as wild and mad and wickedly funny as barrelsful of monkeys.

Graham and Lucy, they both would have been as besotted as granny is. Sometimes I cannot bear to think of them missing her.

THE WEIGHT OF IT

Names | November 2016

Bianca is interested in names. When we got two goldfish I said, What will we call them? She replied Bob and Daisy, without a minute's thought. So Bob and Daisy they are, excellent names for fish. Since then there's a baby in the family called Daisy. And today there was mention of one called Rose. Bianca and I were playing with the notion of having some sisters all with flower names. Rose, Daisy. Violet, she likes that. And there is Iris, next door. And then there's the Bibi plant. What, I say, you're kidding me. Yes, Granny, it's true. She grabs my phone and googles it. The Little Bibi plant, grows well in rockeries, has small purple flowers most of the year if planted in the sun. See, Granny. She has one in her backyard.

She's good on phones. She likes to use mine to text her mother and father. She writes them long letters, no abbreviations, and so many emojis that my screen has a wonderful coloured patterning, like a medieval illuminated manuscript.

Doctor

When she was nearly four I took her to see our lovely GP, Denise. Bianca strode in, said, I want blue 'loves, an examination and a prescription. The doctor was a little taken aback, but found some blue gloves and did an examination. The prescription was a bit of a disappointment, she had to wait for that to be got from the chemist. But she was pleased with the visit.

We do not think of Bianca as filling the Lucy-shaped hole in our hearts. That will always be there. But she fills – and to overflowing – her own space. She, like her aunt, has the gift of love.

Little sister | 6 March 2008

Shortly after nine o'clock in the morning, James rings me up and wishes me happy birthday. He is fond of doing this, catching me before I have had time to start thinking what day it is. He means his birthday, not mine. This is quite a charming thing, to wish your mother happy birthday on your own birthday. And I should be congratulated on his birthday, it was and is a very happy day for me. His birth for me has always been a matter of celebration. I have often remarked that I spent a lot of his childhood working very hard to keep him alive, to prevent him from killing himself, since he was an intrepid child with no idea of the dangers of the world he jumped, danced, tightroped through, and that I succeeded has, not surprisingly, always made me glad.

I have mentioned taking them out to dinner at the Ginger Room, because it is Julee's birthday in a week or so, but say that perhaps the money might be better spent, since interest rates have just gone up again and they are always complaining about mortgage stress. I could do a nice dinner here, I say. He thinks this is a good idea. When? Why not tonight? Okay, I say; I wondered what I was going to do with the day. Now I know.

Today he is thirty-nine. Now I am older than Lucy, he says. He remembers how she used to enrage him. I'm older than you and always will be, she would say. At first he didn't believe this; it must be possible to catch up with her. She was his big sister, but he was determined to get even with her in everything and hadn't been doing a bad job of it. Nevertheless, this was one of those inexorable lessons that life teaches. However much you don't want to believe it, you

James and Lucy on the swing that Graham and I spent hours putting together in the cold and dark one Christmas Eve in the early 1970s.

soon learn that it is immutable, that your sister, older by three years, always will be.

Except not now. Now he is older than Lucy. I shouldn't be, he says, it shouldn't be so. No, I agree with him, it shouldn't be so. We are quiet for moments, under the weight of this.

I better go, says James, who's at work, the phone's ringing and the place seems to be empty.

Don't go to any trouble, he says. Now that she's pregnant Julee doesn't care for fancy food. She's into red meat, at the moment. What about a leg of lamb? Leg of lamb was always his favourite for his birthday. I used to make béarnaise sauce, using mint, for this special occasion. Seems wickedly rich now.

The second scan of the pregnancy shows a healthy baby with a vigorous heartbeat and a lovely tip-tilted nose. The first scan was the important skinfold test, of the back of the neck, which indicates Down syndrome. No problems there. Of this second the obstetrician says, Couldn't see the arteries to the heart very well but I don't think that matters. When they tell her about Lucy she says, Ah, then we better have another look.

James says, But what would we do, at this stage? It is twenty-one weeks, more than halfway.

Nobody expects any problems. It is important to know.

The second scan is the one at which sex can be discerned, but this baby is coy, it keeps its legs tucked together, the technician can't see. It is always to a certain extent guesswork anyway, she says. I think it is fascinating that they can see arteries to the heart but not whether there is a penis. But anyway I would choose not to know. I think the moment of birth with its revelation of the baby's sex is thrilling. But Julee wants to know, and James says, The fact is there, it is information that you can know, why would you choose not to? I think, this is a child of his time speaking, as I was of mine; soon people will always know the sex of their babies before birth. It helps with the name, people say, but I don't think so; you always have to get a good look at a new baby, however sure you are that you have picked a wonderful name for it. I remember looking at James for a long time; he made all the names we had in mind seem unsuitable. Once he found our Penguin book of boys' names, with a paper in it of the ones we were considering. He flew into a frenzy. Oh my god, he said. You can't have been serious. He was quite shattered, but grateful that he had escaped the worst horrors of the list. I had thought of Katharine for a girl, but the three other women in my ward all had Catherines. He probably would have been Olivia. I liked Sebastian, but wasn't quite brave enough: he is James Sebastian. I was very keen on Orlando, but it seemed a bit fancy. But none of these is the horror. I don't dare mention them. I saw very early that they would not do. Their baby girl will have Lucy for her middle name. She will be brought up on stories of the aunt she never knew.

I remember parking the VW in Manuka before Graham and I were married. What do you think of Lucy for a girl's name, I said, apropos of nothing. Yes, it's good, he said. But still we had to get a look at her first. But no time for dithering, with the speedy christening.

This is the month of family birthdays. Graham was 8 March, Lucy 12 March. Julee's father is 8 March too. Julee is 15 March. All these Pisceans. My sister Rosie once told Graham that Pisceans were wet and wishy washy with weak feet. He was offended. There are much nicer ways of talking about these beautiful fish people.

Lucy wasn't hard to keep alive in the way that James was. She was calm, quite tranquil, though also anxious. But you needed never worry about her falling over or out or off or through things. Until that day when she so simply and easily fell out of life.

To become, paradoxically, James's big sister who is now, three years on, younger than he is. He has known this day was coming, has waited for it, would deny it if he could.

My father used to say, Only the good die young. He had a whole ragbag in his head of odd quotations and sayings. Then he'd add, I'll live to a ripe old age. There is something poignant in the notion of a young person, dead, preserved forever fair, not ageing, not wrinkling, not decaying. But it is for us that this is so. Lucy would not have chosen to stay forever at this moment; she'd have thought that living was the way to go. To stay for a long time older than her adored little brother.

Birthday | 12 March 2008

Lucy's birthday. A hot hot day. I sit in her gloriette, which has a small iron bench called a love seat in it now. It's called a love seat I suppose with the expectation that two lovers will sit in it, but I like the idea of sitting in it and thinking of love, which is what Lucy was so good at.

The grass is dry and brown, the tree roots wounded by the lawn-mower gnarl their way through it, there are no flowers on the rose bushes. New Dawn and Pinkie are looking quite flourishing, Pierre de Ronsard is hanging in well enough. I'm not sure about the others. Pierre is from Brenda. Once, Lucy and I were looking at a gardening program on the television and there was a wall absolutely covered with this glorious rose, which she loved, so when Brenda said what could she get I thought this was a good answer. I am waiting for it to take off. I don't think they get enough sun. But then it is so hot. Cleo in *The Apricot Colonel* has a pergola gloriously covered in Pierre de Ronsard roses; fiction is so much easier than real life.

I soaked them with seaweed solution the other day, and now I plan to feed them and mulch them. I might get someone who knows what she is doing to prune them.

All this goes through my mind as I sit on the love seat in the gloriette but really I am just thinking of Lucy, not thinking of anything in particular, I just have her in my mind.

It's not long since my nephew Ben and his partner Sheila and the beautiful Milly left, off to Wagga, back to granny Brenda. She dotes on Milly, as do the baby's parents; who wouldn't? She is four months old, a chubby solid baby, with round perfect cheeks, huge dark eyes, thick black lashes, and a long dark lock on top of her head. She curls up in ecstatic smiles when you talk to her. Unless she is tired and grizzles. Her father carries her around high against his chest so that she faces out to the world, because she likes to see where she is going, but he is also presenting her as a magnificent trophy.

I remember what it was like to walk around with a beautiful baby. You are the queen of the world. I didn't think this at the time, but I see it now. I remember the joy of it, the invincible wonder.

I had such fun nursing Milly, cuddling her, kissing her furry head, her soft cheeks, walking round with her. The old skills available as if by magic. We sat for a while in the fresh morning garden – although the days are so hot, because it is late in the season the mornings stay cool for a while – and the cat, who was fairly miffed that there was another small creature getting a lot of attention, put on a demanding archetypal cat performance, rolling on her back, shamelessly presenting her tummy, having dust baths, sniffing Milly's toes. Milly sat on my knee – she is heavy, you always need to sit down when you are holding her – and watched her intently, fascinated. I looked at her beautiful arms with their bracelets of flesh. Once this was admired in women, now only in babies. Everybody is sure Milly will grow slender and slim when she gets older. Now she is long and chubby. She was after all well over eleven pounds when she was born. Her mother who is a tiny black-haired green-eyed Irish girl was cross because she had to have a caesarean, and had been determined on a natural birth. Sheila has lovely fine white arms and elegant hands; Milly likes to gnaw on things and when she can find her mother's hand she puts it in her mouth and chews it; it is so pretty to see this beautiful child gobbling so happily on her mother's delicate hand. There is a milkiness about Sheila's white skin that you do not see in this country. Irish skins are rainy, Australian ones are sunny.

You might think that having Milly about would make me sad, or jealous. But it doesn't. Though I do feel sad, because Lucy would so have loved to see her. Would have written her cards, sent her presents. James and Julee brought a present. Julee said, I have to warn you, James bought this present, it's a boy's present. It's a black t-shirt that appears to have the AC/DC logo on it, with the lightning zig-zag, not a slash, but when you look at it it says AB/CD. Milly looks wonderfully cute in her rock chick t-shirt, the black suits her, she chuckles her head off. She's got black and white gingham trousers with frills, even more rock chic.

Sheila didn't know that Millie was our mother's name. She said, What about Milly, and when Ben told her she said, Well that settles it, she's definitely Milly.

She looks like her father, and her granny Brenda, and I think a baby photo of me. She sings. There are some Cox's Orange Pippins from the apple trees at Pialligo. Sheila eats away some of the skin of one and then gives it to Milly to suck on. I hold it for her while she burrows away at it, not getting any of the crisp flesh but sucking at the tart sweet juice. Every now and then she comes up for air and a laugh, then bonks her head back down, seeking it out. There is immense force in her desire to suck the apple. She is teething, the apple is cool against her gums.

WORDS AND MEMORIES

My words

I have suddenly thought how very much these words for a dead daughter are my words. Had she been choosing words for her own life they could have been very different. I think she would have talked about her happy times, her normal times, when life was good and she could see it as full of promise for her. Going to school, and the pleasure it gave her, particularly acting. She loved theatre and hoped that it would be her career one day. At primary school, at high school, at college, she was involved in plays. At college she was part of a group the drama teacher collected. He was a passionate person who drew students round him and encouraged them to think about what theatre meant. She and her friend Simone wrote a play about Marilyn Monroe, which they took to a festival in Wagga, where it did very well. I can't remember this teacher's name but Lucy would have done; she kept in touch with him for some time. He wrote to her; Lucy was a brilliant letter writer. People would write to her and she would answer immediately; I imagined them posting a reply and thinking, Oh good, now I don't owe Lucy a letter, and almost straightaway they would because she had replied so quickly.

She was on the school council at her college, and made a good job of it. She was popular, and quite powerful. She loved to dance.

There was school in France, at various stages in her life; she was popular there too and had a lot of friends and went to parties – they were called *boums* – and chattered away in her own French to them. I say her own because she learnt it when we put her into a French school at the age of five. (When I look back on this it seems cruel.

Yet it was a received wisdom at the time, and Lucy who was frequently an anxious person did not seem at all bothered by it.) She came home and babbled the most perfect French sounds and cadences, just as my little granddaughter babbled in English. They made no sense but the accent was perfect. Then she realised that there was sense to be made, and once she realised that she started speaking real French. She was very fluent and successful. The only thing was, her grasp of grammar was impressionistic. When she was older she'd speak the language so well that native speakers thought she was one too, until she'd come out with some grammatical howler which would give them a fright.

Whereas James learnt his French at the age of eight, which is when French children learn grammar, very efficiently. So he speaks with great correctness – as well as freely and slangily – but with not quite so perfect an accent as hers; very good, but not so indistinguishable from a native. (James says this is a myth.) Once, on that later trip I financed by selling the Citroën, we were staying in a hotel at Saint-Flour; workmen began hammering at about midnight. The kids couldn't sleep. I put my head under the pillow and ignored it. James rang up reception, which had gone home and wasn't happy to be disturbed. Neither were we, he said. They suggested he call the police. And in fact it is illegal to do this sort of thing at this hour in France. Instead he went down in his boxer shorts and told them off. They were stunned at this young man who wasn't quite a Frenchman being so fluently and in the vernacular angry with them. They were building a bar in the cafe downstairs and wanted to finish it by the morning. Not on, said James, it was illegal. They stopped.

Next morning when I was paying the bill the foyer of the hotel was full of French people complaining about the noise that had kept them awake. But not one of them had gone and done anything about it.

We had sat in the window of the hotel dining room the night before, looking down over the cliffs on which Saint-Flour is built, eating *aligot*. Blissful, it was, we all loved aligot – a mixture of mashed potato, a lot of garlic, butter, oil and a local fresh cheese, *tome fraîche* (which means the first fresh stages) *de Cantal*. Lucy had worked out an excellent version to make at home; we might have lacked the cheese but she found a substitute that was very good, and in fact hers was a lot better than many of the aligots we ate in France. But the one at Saint-Flour was very good; it is the region for it.

They ganged up on me rather on that trip, complained that I snored. I teased them for being such pernickety sleepers.

A friend of Lucy's at school in France when she was a teenager had one of those bicycles with a motor which are popular in France. A moped. You pedal them and that gets the engine going, to help you on steep bits. She had a spare helmet and used to dink Lucy, and sometimes let her ride it on her own. Lucy badly wanted us to buy her one, but we didn't.

There were twin boys called Pascal and Thierry whom she loved dearly, and they her; she would go and stay with their family. Years later they came to Noumea and called in to visit her (a bit out of the way) and on the Citroën trip she and James had some good parties with them.

At five when she went to school she met a little English girl called Kitty, whose parents were English diplomats. She'd go to tea (*gouter*) at her place, and Kitty would come to visit her. We lived at that time in Suresnes, which is a suburb of Paris, just through the Bois de Boulogne; the school was in an area called Cité Jardins, like the English garden cities of the 1930s. Kitty lived in a very big house, a grand building with a palatial garden, and a French au pair girl who helped with the meals. We had an exiguous flat, in a tall thin house with several rooms on each floor. Underneath us were some people called Fazutti; they were Italian migrants struggling to make their way, not foreigners slumming it for a bit like us. I tried to keep the children quiet but it was hard; Kitty was used to endless room and doing what she liked, I didn't want to be too severe. James, who was two, liked having a visitor and joined in the fun. Madame Fazutti came storming up the stairs and knocked at the door complaining about the romping on her flimsy ceiling. *Les enfants dans les appartements sont des esclaves,* she shouted. Children in apartments are slaves! Meaning they had to be imprisoned in good, that is, silent, behaviour. I said I was sorry and that I would try to keep them quiet. The children called the family the Fat-sooties. I understood how madame felt. Life in that awkward flat was hard for them, but she did go up to the baker every morning and buy fresh croissants for the children's breakfast. On the ground floor were Yugoslavian people, a number, including a young plump pregnant woman, who cooked marvellous pungent-smelling fish soups loaded with garlic.

We worked hard to find another apartment (we were sleeping in the sitting-dining room, and the children's room was a sort of passage to the kitchen; I don't know how the Fazuttis arranged things) and moved to Boulogne Billancourt, also in the suburbs. Relatively luxurious: we had two bedrooms, a sitting and dining room, as well as a big kitchen. It was in an HLM – *habitation à loyer modéré* (I think: dwellings with low rents) – that is, what we would called Housing Commission or Government housing. It was on the thirteenth floor; when the concierge was taking us to look at the apartment she warned me to keep an eye on the children. One day a young woman had left her two little daughters alone while she just nipped out to buy the bread; they stood on the balcony, climbed on chairs to wave to her. They both fell over the railing and landed at her feet. From twelve floors up. We kept the balcony door locked. It was winter, which helped.

One day when we were still in Suresnes, Graham and I were in the middle of Paris, at the bank, which was in rue du Quatre Septembre, in the first arrondissement. Probably having a fight with them, we were always having fights about lost money, it was very good for Graham's vernacular French. We suddenly realised it was ten to twelve, we had to pick Lucy up at school at twelve. She always came home for lunch. We jumped in the car and dashed along the Seine, through the Bois de Boulogne and up the hill. We got there in time. I think of that now: how one would not dream of taking a car in to the city, and certainly would not expect to get out of it in ten minutes. It was 1971.

Graham was on sabbatical, and the French ministry used to entertain us with trips to the country on Sundays to see interesting places and have an enormous lunch. These were organised by a bureaucrat called monsieur de la Forêt d'Ivonne (I'm not sure I can spell this aristocratic name), a tall elegant gentleman who was very quietly spoken. The children enjoyed these excursions very much, even though they meant a long bus trip and a slow lunch. I recall one to Dijon, walking round looking at a mighty statue of Moses and the patterned tiles on the roofs. One of the dishes at lunch was a whole trout, and monsieur de la Forêt d'Ivonne showed Lucy (who was five) how to eat it. He took the fish knife and cut a long slit through the skin, not down the middle but to one side, peeled back the skin, lifted out the sweet pinky-coloured flesh, then the bone and put it to one side. Lucy was charmed by this, and never forgot it; whenever she ate a whole trout she used this method. One of my memories of these trips was walking round amazing places feeling stuffed and somnolent, for the lunches were multi-coursed and the wine flowed and it was very good. But we were young, we managed; now I'd need a nap.

The next time we went to France there were no longer such trips. They would have been expensive and the powers probably wondered what after all they were doing for French culture.

~

The Suresnes apartment was so pokey we had to get out of it, so we would go on picnics. A favourite place was Port Royal. I'm not sure why, even at the time I wasn't sure why. We'd say: Let's have a picnic. Where? What about Port Royal? It was not far away, in the Vallée de Chevreuse. I don't remember that we had anything to do with the ruins of the old abbey, which had been a centre of Jansenism, demolished by Louis XIV and its nuns sent to more conformist convents. We used to walk beside a narrow stream to a wooded dell and sit on mossy mounds amid leaf litter and eat our picnic. The stream had quite a lot of water in it and ran among rocks, it was rather picturesque and blobbed with clouds of foam. These were prettily iridescent with rainbows of light until you realised that they were actually detergent froth and evidence of rather nasty pollution, when they became quite ugly, and you certainly didn't want to go near them. The weather was cold so that wasn't a problem. I remember James in his green loden hooded coat, which he'd inherited from Lucy; I bought it for her from a friend of ours when her daughter outgrew it. Lucy had a cape, which I had made, very cosy, and knee-high brown boots. James thought these were the most beautiful thing and was thrilled when she grew out of them and he grew into them; he walked round admiring his legs with great delight. There's a photograph, with the coat and the boots, and Lucy eating an apple. Rather marred as these usually are by the seat belts. They wore harnesses in the car and we'd unclip them, instead of unstrapping them, since they were not at all keen on putting the things on. We had to have a fight every time, but we insisted, and felt very pleased with ourselves that we were keeping them safe. They could sit in the back, or lie down on pillows and sleep. Of course we found out later that they were hideously dangerous but by that time they had long survived and it wasn't a problem, only a small retrospective irony that what was designed to take care of them could have cruelly damaged them. But it never did.

When we were living in Cambridge we would go to London and see plays. We would drive down, park the car at the National Theatre and get last-minute tickets for matinees. We saw some wonderful things. As we did in Sydney, at Belvoir Street usually or the Seymour Centre, or Nimrod. We would drive to Sydney, my mother would come down from Newcastle on the train, we would have lunch, see a play, then drive up to Newcastle. *Cyrano de Bergerac*, *As You Like It*, *King Lear*; the titles are probably all noted in diaries somewhere. Once, in London, we went with my mother to a play, I forget what it was but it had Kate Nelligan in it, whom I greatly admired; it was a new play and ended with a tableau of naked people. I wondered what my mother thought of exposing my (not quite) infant children, eleven and eight, to this; neither of us said anything.

At one time Lucy's bedroom walls were covered in posters of the plays she had seen. It had a rather pretty eighteenth century–like pale green trellis wallpaper, with blinds in a dark chartreusy green with dark red roses. They'd been there forever and things had got shabby, so she chose to have it painted in an old-fashioned colour called Library Red, very comforting, with mattress-ticking curtains in grey-blue and cream. All the posters came down and are rolled up somewhere.

At some point Lucy gave up the idea of a career in the theatre, I think she worked out it would have been too physically demanding. And she would have had to go away from home, and Lucy loved home. At university she studied English and fine art, and was interested in working in the latter. For a while she had jobs in this area, at the art gallery in the War Memorial (Geoffrey Dutton once called in and she helped him find a picture for the cover of a book), at the National Museum's archives, and at the Portrait Gallery. The last job was part-time, so many half days a week, but they weren't very generous with her timetabling, and she stopped doing it after a while, when she realised she was only going to be employed as a sort of door-person.

She also had jobs in a shoe repairer's and a charity shop, but just on Saturday mornings, when she was at university.

One of her happiest activities was with her friend Leonie's children. She loved visiting her and playing with her daughter, Zoe. Then, when Zoe was about four, twins were born. Lucy offered to look after Zoe, and her parents brought her to our house about ten o'clock at night, when her mother was on her way to the hospital. When we answered the door to this little girl in her pyjamas she said, I don't want to sleep in the bed where Graham died.

This was a single bed in a downstairs room and it was where I was going to put her to sleep. He hadn't actually died in it but she had visited him when he was ill and knew that he had died. So I had to make up a large sofa bed, it was double-bed sized, and she slept in that.

Next morning I was woken by an odd thumping sound. It was Zoe slogging up the stairs to my bedroom. I don't know why she didn't go in to Lucy. She couldn't have tried. Lucy always slept lightly. Zoe said, Am I a big sister yet?

She wasn't, and it wasn't until lunchtime that the news came that she was. It was a long morning for her. Lucy was godmother to Olivia and it was a role she relished; she was a most loving godmother.

Lucy would have told you a lot of happy stories about her life, her friends, her travels; it was only in the last years that it closed down. The operations were enormous interruptions, but they were overcome.

~

I should add that there was a lot of happiness for all of us. It is easy to see it in the times we were overseas, for they are like jewels in opulent settings, they make you recognise them. When we went camping, for instance, when the children were two and five. Friends lent us a two-room tent. We kept the luggage in the half that didn't have a floor, just the grass it was pitched on, the kids slept in the other part, and we in the car, a Peugeot 504 with a camping body. We used to say that it was us who needed the camping body. We had a little Portagaz stove. In Aix-en-Provence I bought a basil in a pot, the potent small-leafed one, we travelled with it between my feet, it scented the car, and I cooked lamb cutlets with courgettes and tomatoes and this marvellous herb; I believe I can still smell it. We had the green Michelin guide to camping, and I always chose sites that were historically significant, and beautiful, with children's playgrounds and not just hot water for showers but for washing up. When we checked into the one at Carcassonne the woman asked, Did we want some bouillabaisse? And gave us a battered aluminium saucepan with this wonderful fish soup in it. The next day the children remembered for years as the one when we had two breakfasts, one at the camping ground, the second in the old town, with its medieval pepper-pot towers restored by Viollet le Duc in the nineteenth century. Croissants and coffee and hot chocolate, that one was. And we bought a plate, not often did we spend money on things, a modern copy of an old faience pattern with a pheasant on it. We hung it on the wall in Paris and one day James remarked that he liked 'that gruesome chook'.

I remember walking round the fortifications of Carcassonne, which were fenced only on the outside where the battlements were, on the inside was a drop to the courtyard below, and the guide telling us more soldiers died from falling off the wall inside than were killed in battle. James was a very strong two-year-old who wanted to walk but no way was I going to let him, I held him on my hip in a vice-like grip while he kicked and struggled to get down. And he is still here to tell the tale, though he doesn't remember it. Well, in a way he does, because he has been told the story so often.

Lucy walked round very neatly and did not give us a moment's worry.

On the same trip we went to see *Peter Pan* at the theatre of Saint Martin-in-the-Fields, in London; we sat in the first row of the top circle with an excellent view. James did his best to climb over the padded rose velvet of the barrier, I had to hang on for dear life. All part of my keeping James alive duty. Hardly had the play begun, the dog Nanna appeared, Peter Pan (played by Dorothy Tutin) flown in, than the curtain came down and a grave-faced secretive manager invited us to leave the theatre as quickly as we could. Lucy departed docilely, holding my friend Marlene's hand, she was always a good girl, but no way was James going to abandon the most exciting thing he'd seen in a long while. He clung on to the velvet bar, and when I prised him off that I had to manhandle him down five steep flights of concrete fire escape stairs – I'd got hold of him round the middle, facing outwards – him yelling No! and wriggling and kicking me, he was wearing his good strong leather shoes. I had the bruises for a long time. And I can still feel the trembling in my legs as I tried to hurry down the steps with this weight battling me. Not sure whether there was a fire or what was wrong. Trying to hold this large, heavy, strong, sturdy child. How well-nourished he was. I do think it was a matter of my rising to the occasion; normally I couldn't have carried him for so long or down so many stairs. We stood in the side street, under awnings, a woebegone crowd. Somebody said it was a bomb, a bomb was supposed to have been planted in the theatre by the IRA. After an hour or two, which I spent reassuring James that I was certain we would get to see the play soon, they let us back in. Both children were thrilled. We all loved it. I think the bomb was just a threat; we hoped so. And I was rather proud of him for being so wrapt in the play that he was prepared to fight so hard to hang on to it. For of course he didn't believe me that it had stopped, that it simply wasn't available;

he chose to believe it was some arbitrary decision. I mentioned this to James just today. I remember that, he said, I remember those winding stairs, going down and down.

Those are perfect memories, I can take them out whenever I like and run their cool and sparkling shapes through my fingers, look at their brilliant colours, the light refracting through them.

Recollections of happiness

Another such memory is going to Ely, in the term we spent in Cambridge. On Saturday mornings we'd often say, Let's go. It wasn't far. Wonderful to be driving across the flat fenland and see it rearing up, the cathedral that was known as the ship of the fens. And it's still called the Isle of Ely, because it had been an island before the draining took place. And Ely is to do with all the eels to be found there. Still. Eels used to be legal currency, and almost certainly still are, if anybody wanted to try it. We'd have lunch at the Old Fire Engine House, delicious English food. In 2014 John and I went in the Eurostar from Paris to London, and then on to Ely, staying at the Poets House Hotel, across the green from the cathedral. Very elegant it was, and had an enormous copper bath, which John tried out. I was a bit afraid I might never get out of it. I sat on the loo and took a photo of it, you can see my black and white sneakers reflected in the side. We went to the Old Fire Engine House again, its blue doors open on to that same village green. I said to the hostess that I had last come there in 1977. Well, she said, I wasn't here then, but it had the same owner, and the same menu. We had grouse, magnificent, and not green and crumbly, which I have read is a way to eat it. There was even a small ball of shot in it. I believe grouse must be hunted, it can't be farmed. I was telling James about this and he remembered well eating there; he was eight at the time.

Nineteen-seventy-seven: thirty-seven years ago from this visit. And I had been thirty-seven then. This seems a magical numbering, but of course it isn't, it doesn't actually mean anything. It's like the fact that my father was thirty-six when I was born and I was thirty-six when he died, a charming symmetry but what can you do with it? Though I once started an essay that was published in Carmel Bird's *Daughters and Fathers* with its potent fact.

We wandered over the green, walked around the cathedral, examined it inside and out. Went to Evensong. Visited the Lady chapel, with its myriad fine white carvings smashed by Cromwell's men. It's a vast space and the light in it is very bright and white too, again because of Cromwell's men, breaking all the stained glass windows. There's a quite new sculpture of Mary above the altar, life size, with long blonde hair, a very modern young woman in a short blue dress, holding up her arms in triumph; you can see her saying, Yay! I'm going to be the mother of God! A great antidote to the stupid destruction around her. It made me think of insurgents in the Middle East, destroying ancient beauty because it doesn't quite fit with their faith.

We went to Cambridge again too, to Evensong at King's, as we used to, sitting in the choir stalls (I wrote and asked, as the widow of a Kingsman) with the seventeenth-century prayer books as big as old bibles, and listened to the boys singing, the most heart-stoppingly beautiful sound ever. We went along Park Terrace, where we used to live, and I remembered walking the children to school, along Parker Street where the great red double-decker buses had their terminus, the pavements impossibly narrow and the fear that you would be crushed, the sweet scent of the washing floating up from Emmanuel's basement laundry, through Christ's Pieces, past King Street and along Jesus Lane, a frightful thoroughfare of roaring traffic and the main reason they couldn't go on their own, and into Park Street where the school was. On the way home I would sometimes give myself a treat and go into Scurfields, the great kitchen shop in Jesus Lane, which I had read about in Elizabeth David, occasionally acquiring a useful implement, and once a vast hemispherical copper bowl, cheap in a sale. It's for beating eggs, and very good it is too, they rise magnificently. Something in the copper makes this happen.

The kids had lunch at school in Cambridge and didn't think much of it. The truly low point was lumpy mashed swede and liver. The smashed potatoes as the dinner ladies called them were always out of a packet. With mushy peas. The meals were cheap, costing as much for a week as for a single day in France, when we lived in Lozère (the suburb of Paris), which reflected their quality. They loved the French meals. Always three courses, perhaps a carrot salad, or some beetroot, or a little piece of pâté, then a small steak, or some veal, or chicken, with a vegetable or a salad, with fresh baguettes and, afterwards, yoghurt or crème caramel, tart, or a piece of cheese and some fruit. Not huge, delicate and well-presented. If you were poor the lunches were much cheaper, but we didn't think it proper as visitors to try to claim poverty.

Our house in Park Terrace, opposite Parker's Piece, was five storeys high, with a basement where the kitchen was (very much a hell hole), two studies, one for ordinary French studies and one for Mallarmé (it was usually lived in by the professor of French who was doing the Pléiade edition of Mallarmé's poems), the dining room on the ground floor, a vast drawing room on the second, bedrooms on the third and a lot of attics. It was a Regency house, and certainly built with servants in mind. Having guests in the drawing room while cooking a meal in the basement was hard work and led to a fair bit of burning. There were books everywhere, even in the little room off the garden which was for doing the flowers. My view in the dining room was of a massive wall of books in the dun-coloured covers of

French paperbacks. The toilet had been retrofitted, cantilevered off the first-floor landing, hanging over the garden, with a fine view of Emmanuel College. It wasn't a good idea when you were in there to think of being poised in space. The bathroom was immense, so was the bath, you could only ever have about a bucketful of water in it, you didn't really have a bath, more a sponge-down.

We were very happy there.

The house came with a cleaning lady who I said I couldn't afford, but I stood in the hall looking up at the grand staircase and the many floors above and decided that we could. Mrs Barker cost 60p an hour. She was another former bedmaker from one of the colleges, and her husband worked for the railways; his job was to shovel snow off the lines. It didn't seem very full-time, presumably he had other duties. Mrs Barker owned the house much more thoroughly than I did. She told me about when they cleaned the silver, and how once a year they took out all the books and dusted them, and when she spoke of these things I understood that by dint of her looking after them, they belonged to her. She knew I was an interloper, perfectly temporary.

My kids got to know the children next door, grandchildren of our professor, and often played with them. Their father was a classical scholar. They lived in a flat in a building at the end of the terrace, not very big, and indeed when the classical scholar decided he had to have a study, he and his wife, a beautiful Indian woman, slept on a sort of fold-out bed under the grand piano. But shortly after, they moved to one of the central houses of our terrace; these were bigger than the other twelve, they had I believe a white wine cellar and a red wine cellar. Useful as he was the wine steward at his college. Our house had a silver room, a sort of safe as big as a lavatory. Nobody kept the silver in it, that was in display cases throughout the house, and the safe had been used for keeping coal. Jeannot, the professor's wife, giving me a tour of the house said it had been leaking and they'd just had the plumber in to have it mended, she hoped it would work. I asked what should I do if it wasn't right, ring the plumber again? No, she said, ring Jesus. Reminded me of the song we used to sing at Sunday school about ringing Jesus on the royal telephone. But of course she meant ringing Jesus College, which owned the house.

One day we had visitors for lunch. Australians living in Paris. One, Jim, picked up a fork and read the label. Ah, la tête de Minerve, he said. He explained that the head of Minerva was a French mark of silver, like sterling (he was an international lawyer, he knew such things). You mean these are real silver, I said. Oh yes. This gave me a great fright. The kitchen sink had no grid, just a wide drain. Like an entrance to the underworld. If I'd known I'd have been counting them. It was very pretty elaborate cutlery, quite Baroque in its patterns. I don't think we lost any, not by my counting after that moment, anyway. There were a lot of family heirlooms in that house. In their summer place in the suburbs of Paris the silver was plated, also elaborate, made by Christofle, but much less scary. In that house we minded the cat of friends, and he knocked a small bowl of blue and white Danish porcelain off the mantelpiece. I managed to get a replacement from Harrods, it cost a bizarre amount of money.

There's a photo of us on the front steps of the Cambridge house, the tiny front garden blooming with daffodils, the children so small. It is such a lovely time when your children are small, so good and loving. All times with children are great, but somehow when they are small you matter so much to them.

There's another photograph, Lucy in her neat red overcoat, with black tights and strappy shoes, with daffodils again, on the old walls of York. We often took such trips, to see cathedrals, York, and Durham, and Wells, the kids liked it because we could buy activities books for them. You had to find a carving of a cat, or an ox, count the number of people in a stained-glass window, draw your own version of a sculpture, all sorts of discovery tasks, it kept them busy and amused. In museums and art galleries they were promised they could choose a postcard before we left; they examined pictures and objects carefully so at the end they could make a good choice. Even I thought this was a bit of a con, all that attention for one postcard. They still surface about the house from time to time, Bonnard's cat on the lunch table, for instance; rather shocking that, a cat on the table, ours was not supposed to do that. Postcards wouldn't work these days, I am always wanting to buy postcards at exhibitions and they almost never have what one wants. I remember wanting to buy one in Vienna, of Lot and his daughter, both naked, him lying down, with his daughter sitting where his lap would have been. I wanted a copy because it was one of the most shocking pictures I had ever seen. No luck. Perhaps they had all sold out.

I think the photographs in York, on bright green grassy slopes full of daffodils, were taken by my mother. We used to tease her about the fact that she always cut people's heads off, but I think it would have been kinder to buy her a new camera. The one she had was a very cheap and tinny object and I think it was the camera that decapitated people, not my mother. She came to Europe and stayed with us in 1978. My father had died in November the year before after quite a long illness. I remember my two sisters and me, sitting in the back of the big black funeral car on the considerable journey to the crematorium (my father believed in ashes to ashes as fast as possible) and making plans for her to come over the next year. I thought that the driver possibly considered it was rather callous of us to be having this conversation following my father's hearse, but it was designed, like the projected trip, to take her mind off his loss. She flew to Heathrow and stayed with us in Cambridge for a while, and then we drove to Sévérac and stayed there for much of the summer. The house in Sévérac had been left to our friend Bernard by his grandfather's cousin, a lady called Berthe. She'd let out part of the house as a small flat to Monsieur Joyes, a lovely old man who told us tales of being in the Resistance during the war and how the locals had talked patois to deceive the Germans. He'd been 'with the waters', that is involved with sewering and providing piped water to the countryside. He knew it well, and took us to amazing half-lost places for meals. He rather fancied my mother, and would make pretty speeches to her which he'd ask me to translate. I found this hard. It was one thing to understand what he said, he had the local Languedocian accent, which pronounces words very clearly, doesn't slur them as Parisians do, but somehow passing this on to my mother was another matter. And then I was supposed to translate her to him. She was very sweet, my mother, she blushed and drooped her head. I always supposed this to be an elaborate exercise on his part, I didn't know what he thought might come of it. Certainly my mother had no idea of falling in love with him and indeed I don't think he expected it, it was a kind of game, a very French game of compliments from a man to a charming woman.

My novel *Spider Cup* is about Sévérac, and the house, with its beautiful linen embroidered by *la cousine*, a wedding trousseau never needed for that purpose. She was such a presence in that house, her tiny dresses in dark cotton with minute flower patterns, her furled umbrella, her sewing machine which was an 1888 model for which I bought a new leather driving belt in Millau, a centre of leatherwork because of the Roquefort sheep, after which it worked perfectly and sewed wonderfully well; I made clothes for Lucy and me. In the book M. Joyes became M. Ange. The core of the novel is the story of the seventeenth-century duke who lived in the castle above the medieval town, who came to believe his wife was unfaithful, and sent her on a pilgrimage to a church not far away. In the forest armed men stopped her litter, and a surgeon opened veins in her wrists and ankles, and she bled to death. The duke built a chapel on the hill opposite, in penance, not because he regretted what he had done but to save his soul. His heart was buried under the threshold, but dug up at the Revolution. I don't know whether she was guilty or not, I liked this perfect story of jealousy. There was a suggestion that he had been away fighting a war when she got pregnant, and a historian could check this up, but I liked the power of the story and its suppositions.

My mother was seventy-two in 1977, younger than I am now, but I thought of her as quite old and frail. She couldn't walk very far or very fast when we visited medieval towns and clambered over cobblestones and up vertiginous staircases. But she did sometimes take the kids to school. Through all those holy streets to Park Street. She'd travelled overseas with my father on a *Women's Weekly* cruise and spent some time in England in the late 1960s, and she enjoyed this different means of travel, living in a place, doing what the locals did, as much as one can. A lot of the old people of Sévérac were very fit, and swarmed up and down the steep streets between the old town and the new, Sévérac Gare, the nineteenth-century railway town; they'd done it all their lives and it was why they were so fit, but we took the car. Our beautiful Citroën CX, which I sold twenty-five years later and took the kids to Europe on the proceeds.

There was a bakery in the old town. You went up our street, very steep, crossed Les Douves, which means the moat, went through the deep arch of the thick wall that surrounded the old town and into a little place and there was the bakery. They like their bread shorter and fatter in that part of the world, the same weight as baguettes but thicker. Fabrice the baker's son was in Lucy's class when she was eleven, and wrote her a note saying 'I love you'. In English. This was exciting but nothing much came of it. She was very pretty, and an exotic English-speaking girl from far away, whereas he was just another local. When the kids and I went back all those years later the bakery had gone, you had to go down to the new town to get the bread. All the little shops had gone. The butcher, M. Rascaloup, who used to kill his beasts in the cellar opposite our house. La cousine had written many letters to members of parliament and such protesting this. The grandchildren of the retired engine driver, visiting in the house across the other street, were allowed to watch, but I wouldn't let Lucy and James, much to their chagrin. Those children leaned over the stable door and gawped. I thought it was bad enough to hear the pig squealing. The sewing notions shop, called Au Doigts de Fée, fairy fingers, had gone too. Most of the houses in the old town are now holiday houses, shuttered most of the year, whereas when we first went there they were full of sprawling families, farmers who brought the Roquefort sheep up the streets from pasture every night and shut them in the barns underneath their houses. Now they have sheds in the fields. Their grown children left to go to jobs in the city and come back for the summer. Some old people still grow vegetables in little patchwork plots, but most have gone to apartments in the new town, where there are bathrooms and running water. Of course the summer houses have all those things too, now.

M. Joyes told us that nobody in Sévérac had been *inalphabète* – illiterate – since Napoleon. The town was proud of this. At school my children learnt a poem, *L'enfant et le serpent*. The child and the serpent. In the local accent it sounded like 'l'ongfang et le serpang'. M. Joyes spoke like this. It was rotund and majestic.

OLD HABITS

Postcards

I mentioned what a good letter writer Lucy was. She used to walk up to the local shops and post them; the post office was also the newsagent, and she would chat to the people and buy a magazine sometimes. She'd met the man whose shop it was in intensive care and it gave them a bond. After a while it closed, a victim of powerful distributors who insisted he stock stuff he knew he couldn't sell, like yachting magazines in land-locked modestly prosperous Hackett. The shop disappeared, and anyway Lucy could no longer walk that far.

As well as letters she loved sending postcards. Collecting them was a hobby of hers. Maybe the influence of that childhood value-adding in galleries and museums. A lot of these were sent to Carmel, and when she came to stay in April 2015 to launch *Goodbye Sweetheart*, she brought them for me to look at. A bundle some four centimetres thick. One I already knew the story of, a picture called *E-Migration or a Flight of Fair Game*, of what appears to be a flight of butterflies rising into the sky from Britain and landing in Tasmania. But when you look at them closely they are women, with gauzy many-coloured wings and filmy crinoline dresses to match. It's the nineteenth century and the butterflies are being imported into Tasmania, a colony notoriously short of women, to provide wives. Lucy found it at the National Library, it's part of the Rex Nan Kivell collection; the original picture came from a Launceston doctor, one of whose sons Carmel once went out with. (There's a sentence.) Carmel wrote a ballet for Tasdance on this subject, but still hadn't done with it, and in one of our frequent and copious phone conversations I suggested she make a YA (young adult) novel out of the possibilities of the narrative. Carmel liked this idea, but when it came to the point couldn't, wouldn't, do it. I think YA is like romance, it looks straightforward but it is something that some people can do and others can't. You have to believe implicitly in it. And of course in typical writer's fashion she did work out what she could do, she wrote a longish essay about the women and about herself and her relationship to Tasmania, called after the postcard, *Fair Game*. It's a lovely thing, and was published in mid-2015 by Julian Davies at Finlay Lloyd, in a series they call Smalls. It's a longish essay but a smallish book. The card makes an excellent cover, cleverly turned on its side.

I examined the postcards, and here is a list (I love lists). Miro. Molière. Kate Greenaway. Old ones bought in junk shops. Books and Writing. A portrait of Frank Moorhouse whom she'd just heard read at Tilley's. Rackham fairies. A Bouguereau Madonna and child. Rupert Bunny. Shoe-shaped ones from the National Gallery. A platypus – 'such gorgeous sveltey velvety creatures', she says. Ghiberti's doors in Florence, two years apart. Odilon Redon, a favourite of hers. Picasso. Escher – an odd St Francis woodcut. Burne-Jones. 1930s posters. The lurid cover, three bosomy ladies in flimsy underwear, of a book called *Spoiled Lives* by Pierre Flammêche; it tells us he is the author of the frank and outspoken novel *Silken Lure* – such fun, 'I love this card', she says. A recipe for stuffed duck's neck, which she begs Carmel to feel no obligation to make. She talks about what she is cooking: two Christmas puddings and a cake. Coq au vin. Tapénade. *Galette des rois aux amandes* (twelfth night cake with almonds, and in it she would have put a tiny china model of the baby Jesus). Peking duck, marinating it, hanging it in the air for twelve hours, serving with Chinese pancakes. 'Lots of yummy cooking' – this written in a Blahnik shoe card in June 1998 – for our thirty-fifth wedding anniversary, including a chocolate cake.

It's good to have had such a celebration, since it was our last. In November Graham died.

One postcard, we're in Bondi, having a holiday. We've seen plays and eaten in restaurants. Sean's Panaroma is utterly delicious. Spotted Nicole Kidman at the Wharf Theatre, walking down its long passage with Ruth Cracknell.

She is going for a slow walk, necessary with only half a lung working. Rosie and Ma are busy editing. 'I am going to buy a few "junky" magazines and feel unvirtuous as I set to on a crossword or two.' She signs off as she often does, 'Lucia'.

She's painting her nails: violet sauvage. And she's reading, lots of that, one day it's Margaret Drabble and AS Byatt. She did her honours thesis on Drabble. The autobiography of Agatha Christie. Ruth Rendell, Dorothy Sayers. Timothy Findley's *Famous Last Words*. 'AMAZING.' Pound's Mauberley stuff. Grimm's fairy tales. Sometimes when you leaf through these books you find small slips of paper covered in Lucy's fine handwriting; notes she made for herself about what she's reading. She's been at the Petherick Room of the National Library, working on James McAuley – this was when she was Cassandra Pybus's research assistant. We're off to buy a drill bit to put up the fallen curtains in the sitting room. I remember that, it was when Graham was very ill, and worried that he could do nothing about these curtains that had come crashing down in the night. But he told me how to use his electric drill and it was very successful, some eighteen years ago and they are still solid. In the postcards there is a continuous underground narrative of Graham's health, he is a lot better, he is much worse, he is in hospital, he is at home. She says 'life is a mysterious and harsh thing too often'.

And she has her own quirky extravagant manner of signing off. Fondest love and magnolia scent. Giggles and roses. Love and toodles and tulips. Lots of woolly cardigans and pots of tea. (The weather is often cold.) Lots of love and warm slippers. A large bunch of daffs and perfumed breezes. Lots of lilies and love. Her warm and loving nature shines through, and I can't help thinking of how much she did with so little; if good health had been hers … well, ifs are no good.

She thanks Carmel for sending her a card of Evelyn De Morgan, remarks that 'it is said she combined the influence of B-J [Burne-Jones] with that of early masters like Botticelli (she dug Flora). At least in this *Love's Passing* Death is across the water; still it's a tad ominous. Yep – the red wings are quite splendid.' She is buying a book, *Regarding Jane Eyre*, and remarks how her heart lifted to see Carmel's name on the cover. She's going to give it to her friend Leonie for her birthday.

She sends Carmel a Kate Greenaway picture of a wicked boy stealing cabbages. 'He's a rather cabbagey looking individual himself, with his burly plump face. An odd card to be among the slim, frocked (not clerical) pretty young damsels that usually bedeck such Greenaways.'

'Dear Pa is at the surgeon.' 'I am still having these palpitations and rushings in my heart. Poor thing: I hope it can manage all these ups and downs. Still the doctors say my heart is not failing me, still I almost believe them, still I'm getting these disturbances, still my back aches etc. So I've begun another tablet. I'm not at all even faintly averse to taking tablets.'

Another card has a lady sitting in a park, 1887, from the New Worlds from Old exhibition at the National Gallery of Australia. 'Dad enjoyed it … [this is six months before he died] but he got breathless towards the end. Mind you these "public places" are always badly ventilated, meaning airless and fetid and one comes out feeling exhausted and in need of large gulps of luscious cool fresh air. Looked at the lake too. I love our lake, our birds, our autumns.'

There is a nineteenth-century collage. Lucy apologises for not making her own, she was very good at this, 'but time is hard to capture at the moment'. I treasure these snapshots of our lives then. This is a month before Graham's death; that night we are expecting Brenda and Fred for the weekend and James in a few days. Granny is staying with us and will go back to Wagga with her other daughter. How busy we were. How much we fitted in. 'These are hard days for us but it is wonderful to know that friends like you surround us.'

Family

Last night James and Bibi were coming for dinner and I felt like resurrecting old habits and making a slow-cooked French dish. James's new partner wasn't coming; she was going to a baby shower for her cousin in Sydney. I hoped it wouldn't have the sadness of the one I went to for Julee; it wasn't that her friends didn't rejoice in her good fortune but that a number of the young women had terrible stories to tell, of prolonged and unsuccessful IVF treatments, of numerous pregnancies that ended in miscarriage, of warnings from doctors that they would kill themselves if they got pregnant again. I say young women but of course they weren't very, not as child-bearing goes, they were well into their thirties, and that was largely the problem. Their misery is something that stays with me. I am always writing about babies, babies where they are not wanted and not where they are, I think it is an insistent theme of the last half of the twentieth century, well, no, of all history. It's what wrecked Henry VIII's marriages. What caused Anne of Austria to promise God a church if he gave her a baby, and he did, possibly with the help of Cardinal Mazarin, anyway that was Louis XIV and not insignificant as children go whoever his father was. I wrote about that in *Valley of Grace*, which was the church in question. Tess of the D'Urbervilles's life was ruined by a baby, Sorrow, whom the priest would not bury in consecrated ground.

And although Julee is not particularly young for a first-time mother everything went very well. Bianca is strong and healthy. I sometimes think that she has the health that was denied her aunt. I can rejoice in it.

I should say that James and Julee stopped being married, they agreed to part, amicably; Bianca would like them to live together again, but accepts it won't happen. She's very thoughtful for a four-year-old. She loves Jenny, James's new partner, and enjoys being at the centre of two doting families, she has two bedrooms and two bicycles, though the favourite teddies are always with her. Jenny is a singer, she and James in their spare time do gigs about the place. He and Julee swap babysitting and they all have dinner together from time to time.

Bianca likes to draw her family: Bianca, Daddy and Jenny, Mummy and Mike with little stepbrother Jasper, Granny and John, Grandma and Grandpa. There we are, all lined up and smiling happily, full of delight. The fact that only three of us actually share her blood is not known to her, and if it were she would not care. She knows a good family when she sees it.

Anyway, dinner: *estofat de boeuf Albigeois*, beef in the Albigensian manner, out of Elizabeth David's *French Provincial Cooking*, a favourite of mine. It's a piece of meat of two to three kilos, cooked with carrots and onions, herbs, red wine and brandy, quite easy to make really if you start soon enough. I chose it partly to recall the visit we made to Albi on the Citroën-funded trip. Our dear friend Nancy was going to be in France at the same time and we had organised to meet. This was an amazing exercise in logistics because it was set up a long time beforehand, and we could not easily communicate after we left Australia, no mobile phones or iPads or emails, though there may have been ordinary telephone calls. She was going to be in Toulouse, we in Sévérac, we would drive to Albi, Nancy would take the train, we'd meet in front of the high altar of the cathedral at a very flexible time. Whoever got there first could just wander about and look at the church. The car was one of those lease things the French do, actually a guaranteed buy-back scheme, we've done this a number of times and it means you get a fine new car. Ours was a Renault Laguna, quite big and comfortable and powerful; we'd actually ordered something smaller and more ordinary but got upgraded. We left Sévérac remarkably early, allowing twice as long as we thought it would take, which was lucky because the traffic was so frightful we were late. We were travelling directly west, on one of those roads that are well-made but of only one lane each way that carry a great deal of cross-Europe traffic. It's nerve-wracking when you are in the habit of four-lane highways to have to overtake by darting out into the traffic, you have to hold your nerve and try not to slow down but gauge the situation and go. James being young and of excellent reflexes was very good at this. But it didn't work on this day because of the volume of traffic, a great deal of it commuters, an uninterrupted procession in each direction. With very many roundabouts. Not to mention a lot of trucks trundling goods around. But we did meet up with Nancy, who was just wondering if we weren't coming.

The cathedral at Albi is fortified. A fortified church is a terrible paradox, this one a huge edifice of rose-pink brick, soaring and impregnable, but now with a door pierced in its fabric. Fortified because of the heresy to which the town gave its name: the Albigensian. It was a stronghold of the Cathars, gentle kindly people cruelly destroyed by the Catholics, who didn't like their religious beliefs. The Cathars thought that humankind was rather evil and the best thing it could do was not procreate and so die out, but they were nice people with it. They were supposed to come from Bulgaria and were thus Bulgars, the word dropped its L and was used to describe the means by which they avoided having children. We had a good look at the cathedral, and the Toulouse-Lautrec museum in the palace where he grew up, with its glorious formal gardens. We had a picnic with all sorts of goodies. And we took a little drive to Cordes-sur-Ciel. This means Cordes in heaven, so named because it is built on a steep hill and is above the clouds, though it has only had the heaven part of the name since the 1990s. It is a very pure medieval town and wasn't destroyed as so many places were when the Cathars were wiped out because it was inside ramparts. It's now a tourist destination, full of craft shops selling all sorts of amazing artefacts, the usual stuff but cheerful and pretty, the town beautifully paved and hung with flowers. We'd been there when the children were small. Usually you park your car at the bottom and walk up one steep street and down another, but Lucy didn't really feel like such a marathon effort so James drove the car up. The street was stepped, the steps were fairly shallow but nevertheless we bumped our way up and it took James's skill to drive fast enough to mount the steps but not so fast we accelerated into things; the space was extremely narrow and full of tourists and barrows of merchandise. People looked at us with some surprise, but nobody said anything. We were the only people making so bold and that would have been why it worked, it was such a cheeky thing to do nobody supposed we did not have permission. I often think of that, Nancy and me sitting in the back of the car laughing with glee while James drove and Lucy gazed regally out of the front seat.

We sat in a cafe and had coffee and watched people for a bit, and then took Nancy to the station to catch the train to Toulouse; when we'd waved goodbye we set off back to Sévérac, very pleased with ourselves that we'd made this rather dicey meeting work, very happy with our day. Going back was easier, not such relentless lines of traffic.

~

The estofat scented the house all day, since it cooked from shortly after ten in the morning to seven in the evening. A way of describing the dish is *boeuf à la cuillère*, meaning that you can carve it with a spoon. And so you could. We had a pile of green beans, which Bianca loves. We had been to gymnastics in the afternoon so she was hungry. She'd had a busy day; at school she had learnt to play chess, and learnt to play soccer. A good day's work, she was very proud.

PS – I asked Nancy about Albi. She thought she might have a diary entry, she didn't, but had photographs, including one that shows the huge pink bulk of the cathedral. And the picnic, with rug and basket and esky, sitting in a park in a place called Villeneuve sur Vère, on the edge of a fountain. Lucy looks gorgeous, and we all look so young. Nancy's memory of the day is the joy of it, which she thinks might have come partly from the implausibility of the whole thing. But there was often joy when Lucy was around, just as there often is with Bianca. The date was Monday 19 June 2000.

Lucy's diaries

When Carmel Bird came to Canberra so that we could have that conversation at the National Library, since she had two new books and I had one that was newish, she stayed with me of course, and slept in Lucy's room. People like doing this, it's a lovely room, very warm, full of sun in winter, with a wall of her books, a lot of photographs, various prints and pictures and all sorts of the odd objects she liked to collect. And the best bed in the house, a nineteenth-century brass Rockhampton bed with a half canopy and an excellent mattress. It can rattle a lot but that is when two people are in it. It's the bed we bought in Kyneton for Graham and me, when we were still in Melbourne after Lucy's first operation. She had got to be friends with a little girl called Joylene who'd gone home after her operation. Joylene's scar was a lateral one, parallel with her ribs, while Lucy's was straight down her front. We had Joylene's address but she didn't have a phone, so we went for a drive in the country on the off-chance of finding her home. No luck, so we wandered the main street and bought a brass bed. Much later we replaced it with a queen size and Lucy loved sleeping in the Kyneton bed. It is very high, and hanging from the canopy she had a painted wooden angel and a pop-eyed blown glass fish.

We do have a guest room but it is full of stuff, a lot of it Jenny's mother's music scholarship, and the bed is a futon, not nearly so cloud-like as Lucy's. Jenny's mother died when Jenny was eleven. She is still full of the pain of it.

Carmel loves pottering around in Lucy's room, dipping into the books, generally enjoying it, and on a shelf she found some diaries. I'd never looked at these; I wouldn't have when Lucy was alive and hadn't thought to since. One is a fat small book, a Snoopy diary, with a page per day, including a cartoon at the top. Lucy was keen on Snoopy. She kept it assiduously. It is for 1982, when she was sixteen, in Year Eleven at college. What a busy full life she led. Early in the year we go to New Zealand, she talks about all the things we did, visiting Graham's Aunt Pauline at Redcliffs, a house that had a low stone wall at the front giving on to the estuary of the Avon. The kids fished, James caught two fish, Lucy one. She made a good friend of cousin Jill's next-door neighbour, and kept a correspondence with her when she came home. She falls in love with all her relations.

At home she is constantly cleaning the kitchen and cooking marvellous food. (I don't need to be reminded of those days and how wonderful they were.) She invites friends for meals and coffee. At the time of her birthday she gives an amazing lunch. She goes shopping with friends, to town, to Dickson, plays cards. She walks all about the suburbs visiting them. She falls in love with the drama teacher, there are kisses and cuddles, very public ones, he gives her the starring role in *Mother Courage*, she has great fun doing front-of-house for

Sweeney Todd. At this time her desire was to be an actor, she hadn't yet discovered that her health wouldn't allow it, and she certainly did seem to have the talent and the ambition. I would never dash any of her hopes. Lucy's heart was such a worry that other things didn't seem to matter. We cared about her having a good time. She gets excellent marks, mainly As, a B or two, only disaster seems to be Aboriginal History. There are excursions, to Sydney for music, to Wagga for drama. She is elected to the student council.

We go to Newcastle, she sees *Macbeth* with a young Jonathan Biggins. We bring Granny back with us. She loves Granny. Granny has taught Lucy to knit and she makes a marvellous Doctor Who scarf, long with multi-coloured stripes. Brenda and Fred, Ben and his brother Kit, come to stay. Granny goes back to Wagga with them. I am struck by how much energy we all have, constantly having people to dinner, driving them home in the dead of night, cooking, writing.

I feel melancholy realising what is lost.

There is stuff about a girl she saw a lot of, who was a very good friend, and some of this she has annotated, briefly, later, when she learnt what astonishing lies this girl told, as things weren't at all what she claimed. The girl was probably a kind of psychopath. She disappeared from our lives.

Another diary is for 1992, not so much a daily kept one as a record. She writes lists of books she is reading, including a detailed account of Ian McEwan's short stories. Exhibitions: Rubens and the Italian Renaissance, Turner. Lists of birthday presents, hers and the family's. It begins with deaths and funerals, Bob Brissenden's New Orleans–style jazz funeral at Queanbeyan cemetery. Manning Clark's obituary. A pasted-in invitation to the launch of *Lover's Knots*, and later of *Wishbone*. A newspaper clipping of me and two friends at a reception at the French Embassy for Bastille Day, captioned: Mrs Graham Halligan, Mrs Helmut Loofs, Mrs James Grieve. There's a dead world.

That of course is how it should be. If I were Mrs Marion Halligan I would be a widow. I will use Ms, but prefer just my name: Marion Halligan. And we look such children in the photo. I am wearing my wedding dress, a short ivory-coloured garment in ribbed Ottoman silk. The date is 1963, goodness knows why the picture turns up here.

There's a letter she wrote when she was fourteen, to the *Canberra Times*, protesting about the killing of baby seals, an excellent letter, which they published. There's a birthday card from Carmel. And a letter she wrote to James, ages before this, when she was just learning to write:

> Dear James.
> I liked you for a fortnight or so but now I don't.
> Love, Lucy Halligan.

There's the putting down of our cat Camille, and the arrival of Josie. Getting Emily Dickinson poems for her birthday. Working at the War Memorial. A record of a full life, mostly happy, with the usual teenage anguish of love affairs. The shutting-down which comes later is gradual, insidious; it creeps.

There's another diary, of dreams. In 1996 we had a car accident, someone ran into us, entirely that driver's fault. She turned right, accelerated, at our green light, as we were driving slowly through it. We were coming home from the cinema, in our Renault 20, a car we loved. It was a terrible crash, and I, sitting in the front seat, turned my eyes fearfully to Lucy, who was driving; her side took the full impact and I was not expecting to see her still alive. But she was. People helped us out and we lay on the nature strip. We were in severe shock, and it took me a long time to get my breath back. The woman did not come near us or say anything, though she was walking around. We were taken to hospital and kept overnight. Graham had frightful bruising to his chest, from the seat belt. Two years later he died of cancer in his chest, which metastasised elsewhere, and I did wonder if the trauma of the accident had anything to do with it. Lucy hurt her hand, and so did I, we both required a lot of physio, something so apparently small but needing a good deal of work, and never returning to normal. The car had to be written off. But the bad thing was she became terrified of driving, she who had always loved it, been so good at it. We had a good lawyer, a friend, and he organised (on the other driver's insurance) to have a psychologist come to the house and talk to Lucy. She came I think several times a week, for an hour, and talked quietly, gently, to her. It was her idea that Lucy write the dreams down. I haven't read them, James has, he says they are very horrible. During this time she had to take taxis, or be driven. One time she was coming back from her friend Maddie's house and the taxi almost immediately had a collision, at a corner. The police let her come home, her father went and got her, and she rang up Maddie and told her. No, said Maddie, it can't be true. Look out the window, said Lucy, and there two blocks down were police cars and all the paraphernalia of a traffic accident. She wasn't hurt, though shaken, but the taxi driver's back was damaged.

The psychologist, a Canadian woman, did a good job and got Lucy driving again, apparently as happily as ever. But I often think of that accident, and wonder just how disastrous it was. And I think about fate. On the way out of the cinema I'd met a man I know, and he engaged me in conversation, not a man I liked very much and Lucy and Graham couldn't bear him. And I think, if I hadn't stopped to talk to that person, rather boring stupid small talk, we would not have been there when that woman did that calamitous thing, we'd have been well past that intersection. But of course you can say that about the whole of life, and it is not profitable.

CEREMONIES

Small candle flames

When I was four I had an urgent desire to go to Sunday school. I believe I nagged my parents about this. They didn't mind the idea but had no desire to take me. They'd been married in Merewether's St Augustine's Church of England, and I'd been christened there, but they weren't churchgoers, at weekends they were busy about the house. My father helped my mother do the washing, boiling the great heavy wedding sheets in a gas copper, putting them through a hand wringer into tubs of clean cold water, the last one with blue added to make the white brilliant. And there was the new garden to make, the sand to remove to two spades deep and replace with soil, so vegetables could be grown.

Auntie Min said she'd take me, not to the Church of England but the Methodists. They were half the distance away, at the top of Park Street hill, which seemed helpful. Auntie Min was a great-aunt, visiting her sister, my grandma. She had a job, I suppose you would call it; she was a lady's companion. She lived with a grand family: the Whites of Gartrell White, the cake and biscuit people. It wasn't very clear what the job was, or why. The role seemed more defined by what she didn't do. No housekeeping, no house cleaning, though perhaps a little light dusting, no cooking though possibly cups of tea, not really child-minding. Changing the library books, perhaps. But mainly the job seemed to be exactly what it said: a companion to the lady of the house. I can't imagine Auntie Min being a brilliant conversationalist. I seem to recall her being evangelical, trying to convert us with visions of hell and my father resisting and there being arguments, which my mother hated.

So, Sunday morning. I am dressed and ready for Auntie Min to come and take me to Sunday school. I'm wearing a blue dress, the colour of cornflowers, not that I knew the word cornflower then, they didn't grow in our salty windy seaside suburb. The dress had a panel down the front embroidered with white daisies, falling quite full from the shoulders and tied at the back with a sash and bow. It's rayon, so the fabric is silky; probably something my mother had in the dressmaking box. White socks, black shoes with straps, a hat made by Auntie Lou, who is a milliner and works at Winn's department store.

Time passes. Auntie Min doesn't come. Nobody has a phone to find out why. I am devastated.

I never found out what happened. I don't remember Auntie Min being around after that. She was probably quite old. My grandmother was in her mid-seventies, she was possibly older. It seems strange that there never would have been any reason given for her failing to turn up. Maybe the family fell out. Auntie Min didn't come and my parents were too proud to ask why but maybe they took offence. I think she almost immediately went back to Sydney. She seems so much unluckier than my grandmother, from the moment of naming: what sort of a name is Min? Where does it come from? My grandmother was Louisa Emily, she had six children and was beloved.

Twenty years after my grandmother died and shortly after my mother's death I found a letter Min had written to her from a nursing home, a sad letter, full of complaint, especially about the woman who shared her room and had only one leg. This woman did not behave well, she wasn't religious, Auntie Min found this shocking. You'd think, the letter says, with one foot in the grave she would have had a better sense of the fitness of things. My mother began a letter in answer but never finished it. At that time I thought, as I think now, why did I not find out more about her, this woman like a put-upon character from an old novel – think of Becky Sharp's chaperoning 'sheepdog' in *Vanity Fair* – except Auntie Min seemed happy enough, she went on holidays with the family and the children wrote her letters when they grew up, invited her to their weddings, showed her their children. How do I know these things, but not why she didn't come that Sunday morning?

I suppose I made a fuss. There still wasn't any question of my parents taking me. I said I could go on my own, I knew the way, my mother had taken me to a kindergarten there, pushing my sister up that steep hill in the yellow cane pram, me skipping along beside. I'd told her about a girl called Kay Giraffe who said I was *spiceful*. I'm sure I wasn't, shy certainly, silly probably, but not spiteful. There was another girl, called Hairnet, I said, who turned out to be Annette, and much later I found out that Kay was not Giraffe but Durack.

So that's what happened: I went on my own, with a note from my father, no doubt in the rather flowery language he used to impress teachers.

I was going to say my father wasn't religious but I've put instead that he wasn't a churchgoer. He had a questing mind and a longing soul and eventually became a Rosicrucian. He loved my mother, and took great pleasure kissing her, morning and evening, going to and from work, that's how I learnt about kissing. You're embarrassed when you're young and your father so clearly enjoys kissing your mother, but afterwards it is a very comfortable thing.

When I got to the church on the top of the hill, with its cavernous hall underneath, it was the Sunday school anniversary, a big day in the calendar, with lots of hymns practised for weeks before, with services starting later and going longer, which is why I was on time. People got book prizes according to their attendance through the year. They found one for me, doubtless feeling sorry for this four-year-old waif sent to Sunday school on her own. It was the *Rocks of Han*, by Pixie O'Harris; I loved it, still do. My copy is lost, but every now and then I go and read it in the National Library, a copy just like mine with some naughty coloured pencil scribblings in it. It was a small paperback book but the illustrations were fabulous and so was the narrative: Han is a fisherman who finds a mermaid, with fine black lines of curling hair long and full as a cloak, marooned in a pool; he captures her and keeps her in a tub, fetching sea water in buckets to keep her alive. He takes away her little red cap so she can't go back to her home. It has witches and a beautiful gypsy girl and romantic landscapes. And a happy ending.

Now I have another copy; Carmel found one for me in a second-hand bookshop in Melbourne, a treasure. Pixie O'Harris was Rolf Harris's auntie, she added the O because she thought it sounded good. Fortunately she died before his disgrace.

I resolved that next year at Sunday school I would get a big book for a prize and I did. Though the big books were often didactic: lengthy tracts barely disguised. I became a diligent Methodist and apt in their ways. I learnt a great many hymns, which they allowed me to sing though I couldn't, and I became thoroughly acquainted with the Bible. Methodists do not just quote the Bible, they give you chapter and verse, quite literally. In the beginning was the Word, and the Word was with God, and the Word was God. The Gospel according to St John, Chapter One Verse One.

We had fun too, especially in our teens, with camps and social evenings and fellowship teas. We weren't allowed to dance, but we played all sorts of lecherous games like spin the bottle and winks, which involved grabbing one another and hasty kisses. Dancing would have been more reticent. We weren't supposed to wear make-up either, all the women had pale powdery faces but not lipstick. We all got new smart clothes for the anniversary. I always prayed that it wouldn't rain so I wouldn't have to wear my boy's school shoes because of the walk up the hill.

In the end I left, but not until I was at university. I left because of the extempore prayers. I could find God in the words of the Bible, and in the music of the hymns, but not in the meandering illiterate prayers that offended my love of language. I knew that this was the sin of pride, that the humblest and clumsiest of words were welcome in God's sight, and for some time I fought against it, but finally I admitted that the beauty of the language was more important to me. I'd read Donne and Herbert and Gerard Manley Hopkins; I couldn't bear to listen to men who couldn't shape a sentence to save their lives.

Of course, the thing about Methodists is that they are democratic – I should say were, now they no longer exist under that name but as part of the Uniting Church – anybody can speak to God. More hierarchical religions, the Catholics and the Anglicans, control the words, they are set down in prayer books and missals, only the priest is allowed his moment to speak extempore. And some are against even that; I think it is Joseph Addison in one of his essays who argued for clergy not being allowed to write their own sermons, but being obliged to get them out of a book of good ones. A lot of people, sitting through a droning tirade, have thought the same.

I have had great pleasure from God as concert, God as towering work of art. The choir of King's College Cambridge, when I sat in the choir stalls of the ancient chapel, turning over the pages of the seventeenth-century prayer books (not just the old versions, the actual old books), listening to the breathtaking voices of boys singing Evensong. Theatres with massed choirs performing Mozart's *Requiem*. Fauré on the radio. Recordings of the *Messiah*. Bach. Such vile things have been done in the name of God, and at the same time such wonders created.

I haven't thought of religion for a while. I think about the great stories of Christianity quite often, the idea of the Garden of Eden, of Adam and Eve and the fortunate fall, especially in Miltonic cadences. They are such powerful narratives they keep turning up, I find them inescapable; their mythic resonances make such sense of the mess we are in. I have a lot of words from the Bible in my head. There's one verse I pull out and shout whenever I see the Labor Party being feeble on the television: Where there is no vision the people perish. That is what is happening under the Coalition and why can't the other lot do something about it?

But what about God?

Since Nietzsche it has been fashionable to claim that he's dead. People keep saying that the novel is dead too and that very evidently isn't true, because people keep writing new ones. God isn't dead for the same reason. People keep writing new ones. Maybe they don't invent quite as many new gods as they do new novels, but there are a lot. At Sunday school I was told that God made us in his own image. We had to remember this and try to live up to it, not do anything that would shame Him. Of course we failed all the time. Now I think that this also is not true, it's the opposite, that we make God in our own image, and we keep doing it. That's why there are so many. And every one of us claims that our God, the deity we create for ourselves, is the one true and only.

'God is dead,' said Nietzsche, and finished the sentence thus: 'but considering the state the species Man is in, there will perhaps be caves, for ages yet, in which his shadow will be shown.'

~

I have been thinking about God because of funerals. Funerals can come upon you unexpected, and require quick decisions. For my mother we had a service at St Augustine's, which she'd gone back to in her last years. We used the old prayer book, the 1626 *Book of Common Prayer*. We had the same service for my husband. And when I had to choose for my daughter I copied his, since I knew she'd want to be like her beloved father. In the church where we were married, the nineteenth-century church of St John's, a small stone edifice built for the Campbell family of Duntroon long before Canberra was thought of. With the same hymns, and leaving the church to the organ playing Purcell's *Trumpet Tune and Ayre*, which we'd had for our wedding. A bit slower for funerals, but the same exultance. My daughter had been christened from that church, in hospital, newborn; after the doctor had said, if you believe in having babies christened I would suggest that you christen this one, and we did, not because we thought she might end up in limbo which is the first circle of hell but because so small a life ought to have some ceremony. And now it had ended, not so soon but far too soon, in her thirty-ninth year, a further proper ceremony was needed.

And again we had the Book of Common Prayer. This not so much for Christian belief as a belief in our own culture, the time-hallowed ritual, the traditional words that people like me have found comfort in over centuries and centuries. The poignant and powerful cadences that our hearts recognise. Language. Not extempore, but an ancient and beautiful work of art and so of humanity. The world is a cruel and dark and difficult place and it is words that light small candle flames to keep the dark at bay.

People were surprised at how comforting and noble and familiar the old words were: Underneath are the everlasting arms. I fear they aren't. My daughter didn't believe they were. But for the moment of the saying of them, yes, there they were, as they had been in people's minds and voices for hundreds of years. With tears in our eyes, for an instant we could believe in immortal safety, the words created it for us.

~

These are the words that John said at Lucy's funeral:

Funeral address for a stepdaughter

Lucy Beatrice Halligan. Born 12 March 1966 and given a few days to live.

Lives thirty-eight years. A life of suffering, and joy.

I got to know Lucy in her last few years, and especially in her last hours.

I knew her as a bubbly, kind, loving person, full of the simple gifts. She struggled with her heart, her breath, her energies stolen from her, but was never beaten.

Here was a woman who inherited the brave intellect of all the Halligans, that her illnesses could not dull. Full of the simple joys. Acquainted with love. An inspiration to us all.

I remember how she would break off from her word puzzles and retort 'Excuse me!' at the antics of some politician or other. How she would coo at the children or small animals on the TV and would cover her ears and close her eyes at the cruelty endured by them.

I remember how she had a close relationship with the ghost of her dead father. How she regarded him as just slipped out for a moment to get another bottle. If and when he returned, she would give him a piece of her considerable mind for running off like that. 'Not happy, Graham', she would say.

As the years wore her body down, gradually, she was not afraid of death, but of a hard dying. But she never gave in.

Her last words to me were: No, I am all right. Mum is all right at the hospital. I just want to get rid of this damned virus. Every day I think I am getting just a little bit better. I didn't get much sleep but I will be all right. I am just going to take a little nap; to catch up with some sleep.

And she died. On her bed, her beloved cat Josie beside her. On her own but not alone. I hope it was quick, quiet, unknowing. Without terror.

She is dead, now, and without pain. It is we who are left to grieve.

And yet she lives. In our minds and in our imaginings.

She is one of those people about whom I can treasure the comfort of having known.

Her courage is an example, her last gift to me: the gift of delight, of life, the love of the classics, of the Word.

Her memory, her example, will carry me towards what we all must come to some day, and having loved, I will not fear.

Oh Death, where is thy sting? Lucy lives.

Wake | 2004

Lucy's funeral was a big party. I sat in my hospital wheelchair and let it all happen. Our family and our friends did everything. I ordered a lot of wine and other people did everything else. My sisters were there, and their children, except Brenda's Ben, who was living in Ireland. Lucy Frost and Cassandra came from Tasmania. Our old neighbours, the Harrisons. Carmel, from Melbourne. John Thompson, from Sydney.

Judy, Nancy, Penny, Claudia. I think they did a lot of the work. Fred too. Wakes are strange things. They are exciting, fun even, laid over deep grief. Both are real and powerful, and I think that is where the terrible exhilaration comes from.

I remember one conversation. I sat listening to Fred, and Lucy Frost, and some old school friends of my Lucy's. Somebody remarked on how nice the funeral people seemed (I want to call them waits) and yet could they really be, since they did this day in day out, could it be more than a rather boring job to them? And yet they were kind, thoughtful, considerate, gentle, had taken trouble to know about us. Fred came up with an analogy. He said it was like a teacher with a group of new students: in many ways they were always the same, but they were individuals too, each lot mattered, you cared for them. The funeral people saw each new family as an individual situation. They persuaded you to trust them. Lucy's friends were much taken with this idea, so was I. It explained how they could keep on being so kind.

It was a while before doctors worked out that my sore foot was gout, and then they gave me some pills which very quickly cured me. The other thing that ailed me wasn't so easily dealt with.

Burial | 2015

There has just been another funeral in the family. Jenny's father, Michael. She has been immensely sad; he was in a quite small car accident four years ago and it left him paralysed. He managed wonderfully well for a while but it had got too hard for him, he had been in intensive care for about seven months. Jenny visited him often and loved being with him, talking to him, holding his hand. The moment of death was his choice, he decided he no longer wanted the interventions that were keeping him alive.

The funeral was a private one at the church he'd attended, where Jenny's mother, who died when Jenny was eleven, had played the organ, with the music he loved, and chose. Jenny sang, so ethereally, so beautifully, at Lucy's funeral. The song was 'Morning Has Broken', and her pure notes filled the church, filled our hearts. At her father's funeral, she read a Lao Tzu poem because Michael was a Chinese scholar, and verses from Ecclesiastes. Bianca hadn't been to school all week, having had an infection and cough that her father was trying to get rid of without antibiotics. She was really better so she came, she was very interested. All of life interests Bianca. And she knew Michael, she loved him. With all the music it was very long, an hour and a half, and she remarked very politely that she was bored, but in fact she behaved impeccably. There was to be a committal at the cemetery and then a wake at a pub. I offered to take her straight to the pub and wait for the others but Bianca wasn't having that. I want to see, she said. I've never seen a coffin, except a glass coffin. A glass coffin, asked James, where? Daddy, she said, with that mild note of exasperation that she uses for the rather dim adults, like Granny and Daddy, she is surrounded with, the glass coffin in *Snow White*.

Daddy refrained from pointing out that she hadn't literally seen the glass coffin, and we went to the cemetery. I realised that at my vast age I had never been to a burial before, though I had seen a lot on television: how many murder stories begin with a funeral, in the graveyard, in the rain, with wonderfully elegant women in black. This was a deep winter Canberra day, but sunny and still. Strauss's *Four Last Songs* were played. Prayers were said and the coffin was lowered mechanically into the deep grave. There were long-stemmed red roses to drop in on it, and then a steel bucket of earth with a trowel to cast the soil in. Bianca lined up for both these rituals. She is fairly sanguine about death, she has known a lot of it, believes that dead loved ones are in our hearts, and she pats her chest. Lucy is in her heart. I didn't throw flowers, or dirt, I did not feel I knew him well enough, but at the end I went and looked into the grave, at the coffin, with the red roses on it, and the handfuls of earth. Bianca came with me and knelt down, looked into the grave too. Bye Michael, she murmured.

John recalled the Seamus Heaney poem, about the particular knocking sound the earth makes as it falls on to the coffin, an odd hollow sound, and there is no answer.

There was something very calm and peaceful about this burial. James was taken by it. Maybe I'll get buried, he said. No Daddy, no, said Bianca, worried, but he assured her, not now, later, when the time came. She told him she would come to that. I won't be there, I said.

~

I haven't written about the deaths of my sisters, Rosie in 2012, Brenda in 2014. It is too hard. Rosie was seven years younger than me, Brenda three. This was not supposed to happen, they were meant to outlive me. I reproach them for this. I keep wanting to ring them up, to talk to them about things. There is nobody to ask, nobody who can help remember. My parents, our childhoods. All that remains are my frail and inefficient memories.

The loss is so immense that I cannot comprehend it.

~

It's May 2015. So late. How the time has passed. My new novel has just been published. *Goodbye Sweetheart*. I had thought of calling it *He Kindly Stopped for Me*, as in the Emily Dickinson poem: 'Because I could not stop for Death – He kindly stopped for me.' My publisher thought this was a terrible idea. It is a book about death and people who read it see this, but they don't find it gloomy, it's quite funny and also there's a sense of good, I think. Death is exhilarating. Sometimes. I have a strong sense of all the people I have dearly loved who have already done it, so well, so gracefully, so elegantly. One would hope to be able to emulate them.

~

My grandmother lived until she was ninety-six. An elegant old lady, slender and spare, she wore dresses of dim colours, with small patterns, and when she went out a coat in black crepe, fastening at the waist with a silver clasp. A hat, fine black straw with veiling. She lived with her daughter Lou, a milliner, unmarried, who retired early to stay at home and look after her. Grandma had had six children, a son was dead and the others had married and prospered and had children and grandchildren. They all lived at Merewether, not far from the beach; they liked to say, within a stone's throw of one another. I used to think of this, imagine rather giant-like people stomping about heaving stones. They'd have needed to be large; as a metaphor it was a nice idea but they weren't in fact quite that close. But you could have walked around and paid a visit to all of them in the space of a morning. Which they liked to do, often walking past the sea and incorporating a bulletin on its condition as part of the conversation, as though it were a character in their lives. Good and rough today, they said. Foam everywhere. Flat as a pancake. Not much sand left. The southerly buster's doing its bit. They'd call in and chat for a while, not usually taking any refreshment. And quite shortly go off again.

The family paid a lot of attention to Grandma and to Auntie Lou. They were always calling in to see how they were. At weekends they took them for drives, the brothers, who had cars. There were often evening parties, at different houses, slide shows if anybody had been away, birthday parties, anniversaries. With splendid feasts, everybody bringing a plate. These continued after Grandma died. My mother told me about her sister May and Stan's sixtieth wedding anniversary. May caught Stan in the kitchen trying to give my mother a cuddle. She never spoke to her again. I think there was a certain déjà vu about it, reminding May of a time nearly sixty years ago when my mother had gone to Grafton to help her with the birth of her first child. I think Stan was into trying to cuddle Millie in the kitchen way back then. I think my mother thought May ought to have got over it after all this time, and not blamed her, she was trying to escape his clutches and at the best of times she thought he was a feeble creature. And now he was in his eighties, an oyster-eyed old man with no conversation and nothing to say for himself, she thought he was a bore. James's memory of him is his telling him how at the age of twelve he smoked eucalyptus leaves wrapped in newspaper. May's marbles were a bit wobbly by this time. Still, she must have felt her marriage was bookended by Stan trying to cuddle Millie in the kitchen. She never made it up with her sister, after a whole lifetime of being excellent friends. Though I think my mother always thought May rather gave herself airs that weren't entirely deserved. We said our mother was much better looking but I don't think she believed us, though it was true. May played the grand lady and lived in a fine old house, though Stan was only ever something insignificant on the railways. He called their house in Grafton Stanmay, which Millie, and her daughters when she told us, thought was vulgar.

I faintly remember Grandma's sixtieth wedding anniversary. I got to present the bouquet. Though perhaps it was the fiftieth. I was very young, the youngest girl grandchild. I also remember the day Grandfather died. I was seven, and walked home from school to an empty house. Puzzling, and a bit frightening; it had never happened before. I was swinging disconsolate on the front gate when my mother came at great speed round the corner, pushing the big yellow pram with the baby inside and my little sister sitting in the front, dangling her legs. She was full of tears and said, Grandfather has died. I remember him, a lovely gentle old man who paid attention to me, sat me on his knee and talked to me. There's a photograph, and I am sure I remember the occasion, the paved terrace at the back of my grandparents' house, Grandfather in his gardening clothes and hat, with a large pale-coloured moustache, sitting on a chair, smiling at me pushing an open-work cane pram loaded with dolls, me wearing a hat too, a big floppy cotton sun hat. I think I must be about two and this would have been when we lived for a while with them, while our house was being built, in their lovely old Victorian house, with the bull-nose veranda, that had belonged to the minister, so my grandma told me, and very shocked she had been when she moved in as a bride to discover it had rats. Fancy, the minister's house having rats. And that empty well that they filled in when I lived there, though they hadn't for their six children.

One of my uncles had a caravan and he took it out to Budgewoi so Grandma and Auntie Lou could have a holiday. They invited me to stay a while with them, when I was at university it must have been. I loved Budgewoi, it was a forest with a whole lot of tall straight trees with round tall trunks going up a long way before there were branches, and no undergrowth, just nipped grass. One day I did a clever thing which I still remember with horror. I decided I would swim from the shop down the river to our camping place. It was a slightly intrepid task of the kind I liked to set myself. I set out and almost instantly realised that it was a dreadful mistake; the creek was full of weed, long slimy waving stuff that clutched at me as I swam, and underneath it was oozing mud. I have a fear of weed, and of mud. Why didn't I swim to the bank and get out? That didn't seem to be an option, I had to go on until I came opposite our camp, and then getting out wasn't easy, the bank was slippery sticky mud and I kept falling back in, I was afraid I would never manage to climb out. Over and over I tried, getting more and more exhausted; I don't know why I was finally successful. I lay on the bank tired out and covered in foul-stinking grey mud. I often thought of that swim, the deception of it, the idea of making my way along the creek and what a pleasure it seemed to offer, and what a nightmare it actually was.

Auntie Lou occasionally lost her temper with Grandma and said *bloody* under her breath as she clashed pots and pans, doing the cooking. (Remember this is still the fifties, women didn't swear then, not so you heard them.) Grandma enraged her sometimes. She didn't pay any attention, she was deaf and didn't need to hear. I was shocked, this was so different from the pictures of perfect equanimity they presented to the world. I tried to help Auntie Lou, I could see that her life looking after an old lady wasn't always an easy one. Grandma was so sweet, but she liked her own way. And in fact I think my mother's marriage may have owed something to this toughness of hers. In one of my novels I have told the story of my father's courting of my mother, and proposing to her, when they were in their twenties, and her refusing him, because she thought he was arrogant and high-tempered. He was upset, my mother was lovely, she broke his heart. He went away and later married a young woman with tuberculosis. He thought he could cure her, my mother said, when she told us this story for the first time on the eve of his funeral, he had read a lot of books and thought he could save her. We knew about Thelma, but only as a girlfriend who disappeared when my mother came on the scene. In fact my father married her, and she died within the first year of their marriage. He was heartbroken, again, tossed in his job and fled away up north, not a wise act at the beginning of the Depression.

My mother told us this story in the context of Thelma's diary. Should she throw it away? Of course her three daughters were horrified. No. No. You have to keep documents. And it is the saddest thing I have ever read. Thelma is so brave, so certain she is getting better, so determined to be well for her Jimmy. And then it just stops.

In a cupboard I have a vast quantity of sheet music. Thelma's. The 1930s equivalent of 45 RPM records, so you could sit at the piano and play the popular songs of the day. I mean to see if the National Library is interested.

After a bit my father came back from up north and began paying attention to Millie again. By this time she is in her thirties. Everybody is sadder and wiser. And another thing …

Millie was trained as a dressmaker. She went to Tech and learnt to draft patterns, to cut out, to tailor. Her mother was a dressmaker too, but she had spent three years as an apprentice, working for a professional dressmaker, without any pay, her only reward the learning of her trade. But Millie never went out to work, she was too timid. She stayed at home and kept house for her parents. And Auntie Lou who worked as a milliner at Winn's department store. I get the impression that Grandma did nothing about the house, she sat and crocheted, embroidered, sewed fine seams, while Millie cooked and cleaned. My father was by now much less high-toned and arrogant, but I think she probably also thought that if she was going to keep house it might as well be her own. So at the age of thirty-two she got married, and I was born three years later. They loved one another very much, though my father was not always easy to live with. But he kissed her, often, serious kisses. I don't think my mother ever regretted giving up housekeeping for her mother and taking it on for herself. Eventually Lou retired early, and made a full-time job of caring for Grandma. In public she was smiling and kind, and if occasional muttered bloodies kept her that way it was none the less an admirable feat.

One day, almost twenty years after her husband's death, Grandma woke up and said, I don't think I'll get up today. And she didn't. This caused a certain quiet furore. It had never happened before. The whole family knew about it, word spread amazingly, though most of them didn't have the telephone. She stayed in bed calmly, everybody came to see her, and the next day she died. Very elegantly done.

She had that elegant name too: Louisa Emily. Lou was named after her, actually Muriel Louie, always called Lou when I knew her.

I used often to call in and visit Grandma, on my way to and from university. She was very deaf but if you talked loudly to her she could follow. I remember these intimate occasions, when I would sit close beside her and think of things to tell her. She'd talk to me too, telling me little narratives. She often referred to the fact that she was the last of her generation; everybody in her life was much younger than her, all her sisters and brothers, and of course her parents, even her eldest son, were dead. So were most of her friends. She remarked that she wouldn't mind dying, and I believe she meant it.

I had gone to Canberra to live, and was married, when she died. I still came to visit her when I was in Newcastle, but of course it wasn't so often. I went up for the funeral, another big family event. I was sad that she would never see a child of mine, but I don't think she would have been too worried, she already had a lot of great-grandchildren. That was in 1965; Lucy was born in 1966.

My sister said I was wrong about her age when she died, she said she was more like ninety-three. Rosie was probably right. She often was. Now that I have lost both my sisters I sometimes think of Grandma and her isolation. I miss my sisters passionately, they were so much part of my life, I talked to them on the phone for hours every week, since one lived in Wagga and one in Brisbane. But as well as my missing them there is the sense I have of so few people left who know me, have known me most of my life. It is as though I am fading. Like a black and white photo left in the sun. John, who loves me dearly, did not meet me until this century. I was about sixty, very different from the child, the young woman, the middle-aged energetic writer. Somewhere perhaps there are people who will remember those incarnations, but I don't seem to know them. My son: I was twenty-nine when he was born, but he has a certain motherly as well as friendly view of me. I once wrote a column about his being like those slaves who used to crouch in the front of the chariots of generals returning in triumph to Rome, whispering: Remember you are mortal, Remember you are mortal. I think children often think it is their job to stop their parents getting swelled heads. Of course the chariot was a joke but like a lot of jokes not entirely. I still know a person I went to school with who would recollect something of my youth. But so much of my past life is lost with my sisters, so much of the memory of our family. I recall some small thing and want to get on the phone and say, How was that? What happened there? What was said then? And I can't, it is all irretrievably lost, my imperfect patching together of the past is all that there is. And when I think of the treasures that there were, which are lost now, I cannot bear it. Except of course I do. What else can be done?

I suppose a lot of people would say, Well, does that matter? Things are being lost all the time. And of course they are. But I do believe that the unexamined life is not worth living, and that an enormous part of that is the recollected life. My parents and all their generation are gone, and now my generation is going too, cousins are dying; what was part of a dense topsoil of memories has been washed away, the roots are loosening, the vegetation withering. I write novels in which certain things are preserved, but nobody anymore, especially me, knows what actually happened and what is made up. But, as my mother would say, 'twas ever thus.

Lucy didn't know about the deaths of Brenda and Rosie. That's a mercy.

Tomorrow is the anniversary of Rosie's death. Four years. The *Sydney Morning Herald* is publishing a review of the book *Rebellious Daughters*, which starts off with my essay, saying I wasn't rebellious, I was good and dutiful and a bit of a prig. But my sisters made up for it. I talk about them a lot. It's a lovely review. My niece Amanda wrote that she had just read the essay, and she was so pleased to have it at this anniversary time.

~

I got an email from Marilla North when the new edition of her book about Dymphna Cusack was coming out. She sent me this:

> Dedicated to the memory of Rosie Fitzgibbon
> of the University of Queensland Press
> whose experience and brilliant editorial advice
> taught me more than I can say
> about giving birth to a book.

I love that people still think of Rosie, still remember her. I recall the day of her christening; I had scarlet fever and couldn't go. Auntie Lou came and looked after me (the maiden aunt, always dependable, always put-upon), there is a photograph taken out the back, on the veranda, with me looking through the window, smiling and spotty. And later, when I was better, sitting in a cane chair clutching a well-wrapped bundle of baby, beaming at the camera, for a change not squinting into the sun.

She became my editor when she left UQP and worked as a freelancer, from *The Apricot Colonel* to *Shooting the Fox*. She was so good. We used to argue about commas; she'd say I'm the editor, Marion, and it is my job to tell you about these things, but you're the writer and you can ignore me if you wish. Once we spoke together to the Society of Editors and I mentioned this; she denied she'd ever said it. But I am sure she did, or words to that effect. Sometimes I took her advice about the commas but sometimes I couldn't. She rang me up about *The Apricot Colonel* and I could tell she was in great fear and trembling. I think you should lose the first chapter, she said. She'd have been glad she was on the phone, at some remove from my wrath. Oh yes, I said, yes, I think you're right. She was dumbfounded, but she was right, and anyway losing the first chapter isn't anything like as drastic as changing a comma. It turned into a brief paragraph of prologue which is a much better idea.

Sometimes we irritated Brenda when the three of us were together because we talked shop so much, but mostly we just had a great time. Like my seventieth birthday, up the Hunter Valley. It seemed as though those good times would go on all my life.

It breaks my heart that they are gone.

THE COLOUR OF TRUTHS

Poems

Kate Llewellyn dedicated a book of poems to Lucy, and Alan Gould wrote this one for her. He sent it to us with this note:

> Marion, John,
> The postmaster tells me that my effort to send you the poem below failed yesterday. Here is another try. I run it past you for discretion's sake, hoping you will not mind my reference to Lucy.
> All the best for Christmas and the New Year, Alan

I Try to Think that Vile Thing Down

Today I heard they've killed Margaret Hassan,
having first filmed her pleading for her life,
this without dignity on willing Arab television.
For thirty years she helped the Baghdad poor,
and now, one side or other has murdered her,
having first made her kneel to babble pleas
abject and irrelevant to her good deeds.
For her killers I wish them the Soviets in Beirut.
We find you, take you to the cellars
where whimper and bravado have no viewers,
we tell you plainly you are to be shot,
your genitals cut from your bodies,
and delivered by post to your families.
Ten minutes of your life remain.
Whereon the business was done,

one, and one, and one.
And look how my wish defiles the long good will
of Margaret Hassan's existence in the world.
Look how she turns her face from me in horror.
And just today I sat at the funeral
of a brave, cheerful girl who died at last
having lived decades next to death
where charity for her was simple breath,
who, tubed to oxygen would do
her wordgames before the TV news,
would glance and quizzically exclaim
Well excuse me! when some big shot name
advocated folly or cruelty.
And look how she,
content beside the reptile-quick TV
has also made her presence tell
beside the small and vile
defilers of good will.

~

Eventually I did come to write stories about Lucy's experiences. They are fiction but fiction is always life. One came out of Lucy's stay in the cystic fibrosis ward. I was having lunch in Carlton and met one of the nurses, he was a lovely man, so good to the kids, so warm, so kind. He said he was taking a short break with his lover and going on a holiday. He talked about it quite a lot and I realised I had no idea whether this lover would be a man or a woman and I liked this idea. I had him stand on the balcony and look out on Gatehouse Street, as I had done at Ronald McDonald House, watching the trucks passing, stopping, starting, grinding away, and as I thought of them then a great many of the words came from Matthew Arnold's 'Dover Beach'. The 'melancholy, long, withdrawing roar', 'the breath of the night-wind', the 'grating'. Images of desolation and abandonment. The poem was running through my mind … Ah love, let us be true to one another … But I doubt anybody would notice it who was not expecting it.

Another story was a conflation of Lucy's two operations. Ronald McDonald House and the terrible narratives it housed came from the second one. But the children and their operations and especially not surviving them came from the first. It took me a long time to be able to write about it. I needed it to be a long time in the past. The story is called 'Here Be Unicorns' and one of the things in it is the need of the parents of these children to keep giving them presents. A sort of atavistic act, as though the survival of these material objects will rub off on the kids. The unicorn was a tubby little glass figurine, but as an image it had quite a lot of weight. And I was particularly intrigued with the idea of tattoos and scars. Many of the residents had tattoos, and, as I've said, I was fascinated by the difference between these beautifully drawn scars, so delicate, so precise, and the cobbled rough stitching of the massive scars down the chests of their little ones. The house wasn't just for poor people but a lot of them were. Their main response was puzzlement, they did not understand this cruel thing that was happening to them, they could not believe that their child was going to die. This narrative belongs to a past time, the 1970s, when tattoos were much rarer than they are now, in fact considered rather louche, and not common in women. There was a young couple living in the house, with a very sick baby. The man had a lot of tattoos on his thin arms and chest, and I wondered whether when he had them done he imagined himself strong and muscular. They wore singlets and tracksuits and broken down moccasins with fur linings folded over the outside. They came from Tasmania and they had a lot of time because they were on the dole. Not just for the time of the operation but always. I remember coming in late one evening, after being with Lucy, and they were sitting in the lounge with big mugs of instant coffee watching a movie with subtitles. Except of course they weren't watching it, it was playing on the screen in front of them and they were sunk in misery and not at all aware of what their eyes gazed on. Normally they'd have changed to a commercial channel but somehow they couldn't do this. It was as though a movie with subtitles was just another fate. The doctor had told them that the next day was the time to turn their baby's life support system off; they couldn't believe that their hope had come to this. All the clever operations (seven in all, in six months), all the care, the attention, the intensive nursing, and their baby was scheduled to die. They sat on the sofa saying the same bewildered things over and over.

It is strange, being companion to the grief of others. It reminds you of this horror for yourself: will my child be in the same situation? But there is another terrifying aspect to it. Maybe in the huge and terrible game of odds in life, this child dying means that fate intends yours to live. You don't want to think this, but it comes into your mind, and there you are, thinking it. You know that fate doesn't work like this, but there you are, thinking it.

The passage of time

It's a funny thing, when a doctor tells you to have your child christened because it is expected to die. It changes your life, everything afterwards is different. Even though in Lucy's case this didn't happen as immediately as they feared, she managed her thirty-eight years, but it did happen. It was a bit like a bad fortune, or a curse, the wicked fairy at the christening, you could choose not to believe it, try to forget it, nevertheless it is there, always hanging, always glooming, lurking ready to catch you at pleasant unaware moments. I'm reminded of my novel *The Point*, where a clever teenager, a hacker, is accidentally killed by a drug overdose, and his mother is obscurely aware that in some ways it is a relief, that this thing she had feared for so long has happened, so she does not have to worry about it anymore. (This story came from my sister Rosie; it happened to the mother of a friend of her son's.) It is fifty years since my curse was pronounced, and twelve years that I ought to have been free of it, but somehow it remains, no longer possible but still somehow potent. The worry, the fear, the panic: yes, I know the things they signalled won't happen now, since they already have, but their force isn't lost. But then, there also remains my joy in having had Lucy for those thirty-eight years.

My dear child, these words are for you, and though I have no expectation you will ever have any consciousness of them, yet you are alive in them, as vital I hope as you were in life.

And now there is another beautiful baby, and very healthy, this one. Edgar James Halligan, named after his great-great-grandfather, Edgar Sawer, a hero of the First World War, who received his military cross from the hands of the King himself. New Edgar has fine smooth skin and the handsomest round head. I have a photo of my mother as a baby, of Lucy, of Bianca, and they all have this elegant round head. Spanning the generations. He smiles at his mother. And his father, laughs, tries to talk, squeezes his chest and waves his hands, you can see he believes that if he just tries hard enough out will come words. And of course, one day they will. Bianca reads him her favourite books, and sings nursery rhymes to him. She loves him, and he her. And I am so sad that his grandfather, his aunt, his great-aunts, will never know him.

Another thing, before I finish

When I write a memoir I want it to be true. But this is already tricky. Anything I write has to be true, but truths can be different. Facts are another matter.

I am imagining this picture I am sketching for you, the small family with its moments of intense sorrow and then the other side of that is bliss. But there is some sorrow that I have never put in and that was when Graham broke my heart. He tried to mend it again but I'm not sure that can be done. Humpty Dumpty things, hearts, can't be put back together again. Still, there was a lot of trying.

The breaking was when Graham got besotted with a rather young woman. He'd have said that he still loved me but in her was this irresistible lure. I can see it was fairly much my fault, that I trusted him so completely, had such faith in him, that I had no fear when he introduced this young woman, babysitter, student, admirer of our ways, craver of our manners, desirer of my life and of my husband to make it with. Of course it wasn't going to happen, we were safe, it was me he loved, but she, we'll call her Cee, didn't go away. However much he promised that she had.

I don't talk of this much, except in fiction, and there I make fiction out of it, making what I will of it. Readers of my novels will recognise bits. In life it was horrible. One night I so hated it that I jumbled a whole lot of his things in a couple of suitcases and threw them down the stairs. There, I shouted, you can get the rest later. He was not happy with this, but finally went, in one of our old Holdens, leaving me the Citroën. She was thrilled, I know, it was what she wanted. (Well, she'd have liked the Citroën as well.) Not what I wanted, I wanted life with him, not turning up odd corners and finding her installed.

He went to her flat, and lived with her, just round the corner from me. And then odd things happened. He started ringing me up. So many important things to talk about. The gas bill, the electricity. The kids' schooling. The insurance. Too much to discuss on the phone. We should have lunch and work them out. Having been very innocent at the beginning, I now became crafty. I quite liked having adulterous lunches with my husband, who began to court me. Buying my favourite wine. Stroking his index finger along the back of my hand. He told me that he pretended to be asleep in the morning, so she got dressed quietly and went to work without talking to him. I felt quite sorry for her. No I didn't. He invited me for a drink so he could tell me about his terrible dreams, of the house burning down and him trying to break in and save us. Of a murderer with an axe trying to smash his way in. He could read these dreams, he knew that he was the danger to the safety of the family he was trying to preserve. He thought he should come back home and look after us. I got quite good at not saying much. I was quiet, and looked into the distance.

One afternoon, evening really, he called in with a bottle of chianti. Colli Senesi, the hills of Siena. Remember, he said. I did. The kids were quite pleased to see him. Yes Mum, they said. What are you having for dinner? Pizza? Oh good, I'll get it. Eventually he rang her up and said he'd had rather a lot to drink and wouldn't be driving back that night. I made him sleep in the spare room. At first. He went and got his things. I don't know what he said to her.

When he was dying he said I was the love of his life. And yes, I believed him.

So the idyllic family is true sometimes. But then I suppose it always is. Most of the time, in this case, and not something he could give up.

I often think about Cee. I imagine her as a kind of mid-life crisis. If his career was a bit bumbling then there was a juicy love affair. I thought she was silly to hang around as long as she did, when it was clear nothing would happen. Eventually she got married and had a little girl, who died apparently without rhyme or reason at twelve days old. Graham went to the funeral. In times of sadness you do what you must.

And I certainly got a lot of narratives.

In *The Taste of Memory* I wrote about gardens, how people create their own small paradises to dwell in, to make life pleasant. A lot of us make gardens for ourselves, even if it is only some pots on a balcony. And I said that the thing about paradises is that they often have a serpent in them. And I thought that ours did. Not Lucy's illness, that was not a serpent, it was fate, something inexorable that just was. Whereas with serpents there is an element of choosing. Graham chose to invite the serpent Cee into our lives, and very hard she was to get rid of. But finally we did. Out of the garden, anyway.

~

Well. There it is. I've never actually written that before. I've fiddled about with it, danced around it, played with it, but I've never told the plain unvarnished tale before. It's only memoir's desire for honesty that gets me telling it now. It's funny how people don't believe you about the making of life into fiction. I remember when I wrote *The Fog Garden*, which says on the front cover that it is a novel, and believe me I would know, there was no way I was going to practise the honesty of memoir there, I was somewhat enraged to be informed that one of the judges of the Miles Franklin Award disqualified it on the grounds that it was not a novel. Now some of its narratives fell complete into my hands, like coming home from hospital late after visiting Lucy, turning the television on and finding the story of Eva Peron, whose embalmed body got into the clutches of one of her enemies and was kept standing in a corner of his office and used for necrophiliac purposes. I'm not sure if his intention was pleasure, or revenge. Both I suppose. It makes a good story of sex and death, which is very much what *The Fog Garden* is about. But such givens hardly make it not a novel. Think of *Jane Eyre*, or *David Copperfield*; those writers used their lives but in all sorts of imaginative ways. Wherever else is a novel going to come from?

POSTSCRIPT

I was watching the *Antiques Roadshow*, which I enjoy for its narratives. So many strange stories attached to objects, which may be beloved or just stuff. This episode was from Winchester Cathedral. Jane Austen spent her last days in Winchester, she died there at the age of forty-one and was buried in the cathedral. Her memorial says all sorts of good things about her but doesn't mention that she wrote any books. The presenter of the program quoted her sister Cassandra's words:

> I have lost a treasure, such a sister, such a friend as never can have been surpassed. She was the sun of my life, the gilder of every pleasure, the soother of every sorrow, I had not a thought concealed from her, and it is as if I had lost a part of myself.

I cried when I heard this; fancy, sitting weeping to the *Antiques Roadshow*. But it was so exactly how I feel about my sisters, and about my daughter – the right words will always make me cry. And I thought that grief is like a fountain, whether it is an elaborate carved stone affair or a simple basin: however dry and dusty it seems, there is always a switch that will set the water flowing again.

~

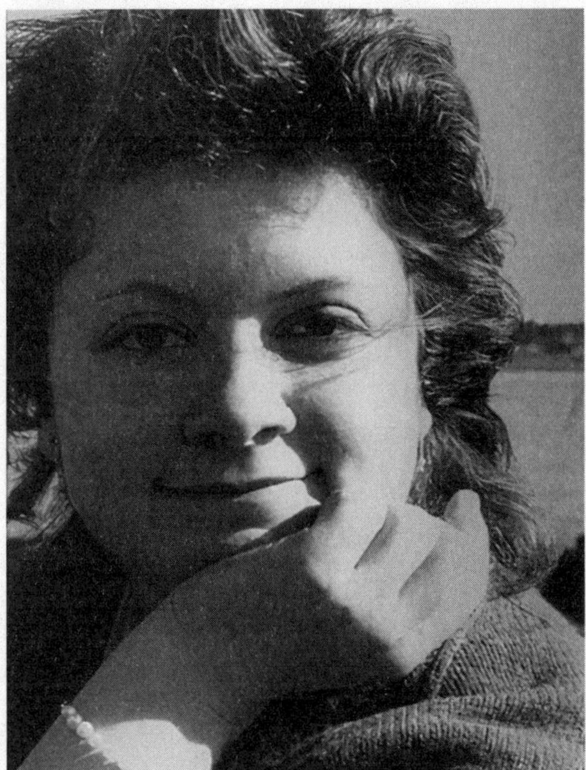

This image was given to James by Damian McDonald of the National Library at the time of Lucy's death. The portrait was taken from a larger group image as a gift to the family.

CREDITS

The poem 'Puzzled Light' by David Brooks on pages 90–2 is reproduced with permission.

'Small candle flames' on pages 181–7 is an abridged version of an essay of mine that was originally published in *Griffith Review*, for an issue about religion in 2009.

The Nietzsche quote on page 186 is from *The Gay Science* by Friedrich Nietzsche, first published in 1882.

The funeral address by John Stokes on pages 188–9 is reproduced with permission.

The poem 'I Try to Think that Vile Thing Down' by Alan Gould on pages 205–6 is reproduced with permission.

Marion Halligan AM is an Australian writer and novelist. She has served as chairperson of the Literature Board of the Australia Council and the Australian National Word Festival. She was appointed Member of the Order of Australia (AM), General Division, in 2006 for services to literature and for her work in promoting Australian writing. Her published works include:

Novels

The Apricot Colonel
The Fog Garden
The Golden Dress
Goodbye Sweetheart
Lovers' Knots: A Hundred-Year Novel
Murder on the Apricot Coast
The Point
Self Possession
Spider Cup
Valley of Grace
Wishbone

Non-fiction

Cockles of the Heart
Eat My Words
Out of the Picture
The Taste of Memory
Those Women Who Go To Hotels

Plays

Gastronomica

Short story collections

Collected Stories
The Hanged Man in the Garden
The Living Hothouse
Shooting the Fox
The Worry Box

Children's

The Midwife's Daughters

Marion has also edited two titles, *The Gift of Story: Three Decades of UQP Short Stories* and *Storykeepers*, and contributed three stories to *Canberra Tales: Stories.*